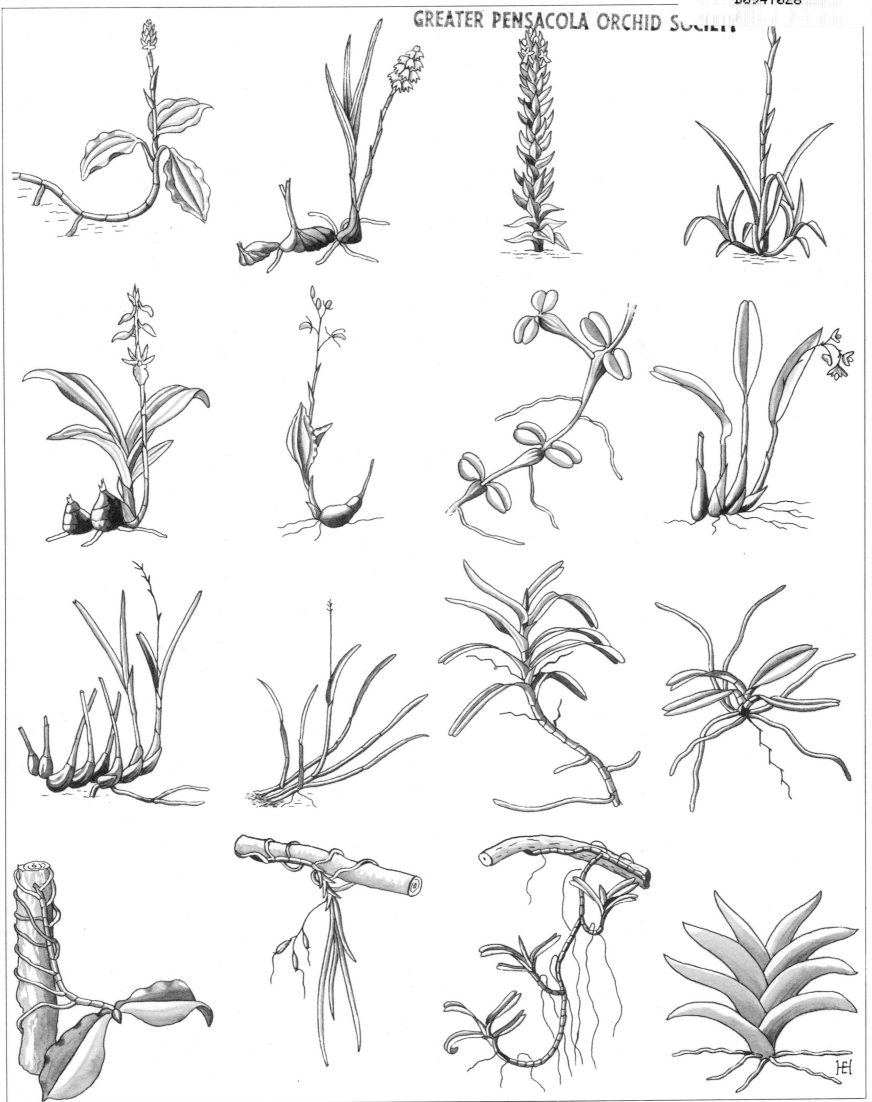

Orchids of Africa

E. F. Hennessy

Orchids of Africa

A Select Review

Text by J. Stewart

Illustrations by E. F. Hennessy

HOUGHTON MIFFLIN COMPANY
Boston

Published in 1981 by
THE MACMILLAN PRESS LTD
London and Basingstoke

Published in the United States and Canada by
HOUGHTON MIFFLIN COMPANY

Library of Congress Cataloging in Publication Data

Stewart, Joyce.
  Orchids of Africa

    Bibliography: p.
    Includes index.
    1. Orchids — Africa, Sub-Saharan. I. Hennessey, Esmé
Franklin, 1933–   . II. Title.
QK495.O64S72   584'.150967   81-6589
ISBN 0-395-31771-1   AACR2

Text set in 13/16 pt Garamond
Printed in Hong Kong

Contents

Illustrations

Preface

In Europe and America, Asia and Australia, the indigenous orchids look very different from the plants portrayed in this book. In every continent's characteristic orchid flora, the flowers of the individual species and genera share a simple basic pattern, but they all differ in detail. There is more diversity than man could possibly have invented, even in the age of the computer. Nevertheless, there is such an overall similarity, a family likeness, that the visitor or newcomer, interested in orchids but knowing nothing of African genera, will find our plants familiar at once but also somewhat strange. This introductory volume has been produced to illustrate something of the character, construction and charm of the intriguing orchids of Africa.

Because of the curious mystique that orchids enjoy, their detailed structure is often unknown, disregarded, or misunderstood. In the first part of this book, the peculiar features of the plants and flowers of African orchids are described and illustrated in an extensive review of their characters. The botanical terms are presented in perspective and are further defined in a glossary at the end of the book. This review is, necessarily, selective, but may facilitate the identification of species and genera in technical texts and floras, in which a knowledge of terms is frequently assumed. At the same time, it should promote an understanding of relationships, both within the orchid flora of Africa and with genera and species of other continents. It is hoped that it may also prove of value to orchid lovers in Africa, many of whom have always known which orchid is which, but have never been able to find out why.

In the second part of the book fifty different species are illustrated, described and discussed in detail. They have been selected to depict some of the diversity of plant habit, inflorescence form and flower structure that can be found among the African orchids. It is hoped that this small selection, less than five per cent of the total orchid flora, will provide a tantalizing introduction to the unique, elegant and beguiling orchids of this continent.

Many people have helped us, sometimes unknowingly, in assembling the material used in the preparation of this book. We thank them, and acknowledge their help in the appropriate places in the text. Where no source is mentioned, the plants have been collected and grown by the author. We wish to thank our typists, Marjory Hill, Joan Henderson and Beulah Girdwood. We particularly wish to thank Lieutenant Commander B.J. Hennessy who, on many occasions, has transported plants between the author in Pietermaritzburg and the artist in Durban. We also wish to thank Eleanor-Mary Cadell, of Macmillan South Africa, for her interest, enthusiasm, patience and help in the realisation of this project.

PART I
A Review of the African Orchids

'Among the manifold creatures of God that have all in all ages diversely entertained many excellent wits, . . . none have provoked mens studies more, or satisfied their desires so much as plants have done, and that upon just and worthy causes: for if delight may provoke mens labor, what greater delight is there than to behold the earth apparelled with plants, as with a robe of embroidered worke, set with Orient pearles and garnished with great diversitie of rare and costly jewels? . . . the principal delight is in the mind, singularly enriched with the knowledge of these visible things . . .

There be divers kindes . . . [of orchids] differing very much in shape of their leaves, as also in floures: some have floures, wherein is to be seen the shape of sundry sorts of living creatures; some the shape and proportion of flies, in other gnats, some humble bees, others like unto Honey bees; some like Butter-flies, and others like Waspes that be dead; some yellow of colour, others white; some purple mixed with red, others of a browne over-worne colour: . . . there is not any plant which doth offer such varietie unto us as these . . .'

John Gerard, 1597
The Herball or Generall Historie of Plantes

Introduction

One hundred different genera of orchids are known from the part of the African continent that lies south of the Sahara. Over half of these are never found beyond its shores, and a further quarter is found, elsewhere, only on the nearby islands of the western Indian Ocean. Thus at least three-quarters of the genera are unique to the Afro-Malagasy region. They are not only unique, but characteristic, comprising whole subtribes of the orchid family that are endemic to this area. They display varied growth patterns and complex flowers with a great diversity of colours, structures, scents and size. Many are distinguished by their prolific flower production and ease of culture, while others remain rare and recalcitrant, reluctant to bloom either in the wild or in cultivation.

A list of the orchid genera recognised in Africa is not difficult to compile, but the number of different species within many of the genera is still a matter for conjecture and estimation. The small, distinctive genera containing one species, or only a few, are mostly well known, but in all those with ten species or more it is extremely likely that there are others, undiscovered and undescribed as yet, in remote mountain habitats throughout the continent, but particularly in the tropics.

Fairly accurate totals are available for certain areas, including South Africa (434), Kenya (247), West Tropical Africa (401), Zaïre (414), Zambia (398) and Zimbabwe (340), but a total for the whole continent is not just a matter of simple addition of these and other figures. For some large areas, such as Tanzania, Uganda, Ethiopia, and Congo (Brazzaville), no check-lists have been compiled. Some orchid species have widespread distributions and their names appear in all the existing lists, whereas other species may also appear in each list but disguised by different names in each one. Taxonomic revision on a continental basis frequently reduces the number of names that are applied to a single species to only one that is valid, but at the same time new species are being discovered and described almost continuously. So the overall number of species that may be present is certainly more than one thousand, probably in the region of 1500, but this figure is very tentative and will be subject to fluctuations for many more years while careful comparative work is being carried out.

Compared with the numbers of orchid species recorded in South America, this figure is almost incredibly small. But it is perhaps more sensible to compare the African continent with Australia, the third great land mass in the southern hemisphere, where the number of orchid species so far recorded is only half of the total for Africa. Huge areas of both these continents are dry enough to be described as desert, or semi-desert, or are only irregularly moist enough to support the seasonal growth of perennial plants. Thus orchid plants find that many parts of the African continent provide inhospitable conditions which are inimical to their existence or spread, because they depend on an association with a fungus that lives only in moist conditions for the germination of their seeds, because they need a good supply of moisture during the growing season, and because a host plant that provides a growing site is essential to epiphytic species. While there are some favourable areas that are rich in species flowering for at least three or four months of the year, there are also huge tracts of country where orchids are very rare plants indeed, if not entirely absent.

In selecting the fifty species that are illustrated and discussed in detail in the second part of this book, we have chosen those that best display some of the variety of vegetative and floral form that is characteristic of the orchids of this region. Two tribes, the Orchideae and the Vandeae, comprise an overwhelming proportion of the total genera and species, and within each of these there is some similarity of basic growth pattern.

But, in contrast, there is tremendous diversity in design, colour, size and arrangement of the flowers. Sixteen representatives of each of these tribes provide an introduction to these typically African orchids. The remaining eighteen species have been selected from another six tribes, all of which have members in other parts of the world as well as some striking representatives in Africa.

A Record of the Orchidaceae in Africa

The order in which the tribes and subtribes are listed is the same as that of Dressler (1974), whose classification within the orchid family is followed in this book.

TRIBE	SUBTRIBE	GENUS	APPROX. NUMBER OF SPECIES
Neottieae Lindley	Limodorinae Bentham	*Epipactis* Zinn	2
Cranichideae Endlicher	Corymbidinae Miquel	*Corymborkis* Thouars	1
	Spiranthinae Lindley	*Manniella* Reichenbach *fil.*	1
	Goodyerinae Klotzsch	*Cheirostylis* Blume	2
		Hetaeria Blume	5
		Platylepis A. Richard	1
		Zeuxine Lindley	3
Epipogeae Parlatore		*Epipogium* R. Brown	1
Orchideae	Orchidinae	*Stenoglottis* Lindley	3
		Cynorkis Thouars	15
		Habenaria Willdenow	200
		Bonatea Willdenow	20
		Platycoryne Reichenbach *fil.*	17
		Roeperocharis Reichenbach *fil.*	5
		Centrostigma Schlechter	3
		Holothrix Lindley	50
		Bartholina R. Brown	2
		Neobolusia Schlechter	4
		Schwartzkopffia Kraenzlin	2
		Brachycorythis Lindley	20
		Schizochilus Sonder	10
		Huttonaea Harvey	5
	Disinae Bentham	*Schizodium* Lindley	6
		Disa Bergius	113
		Monadenia Lindley	16
		Herschelia Lindley	17
		Brownleea Lindley	6
		Pachites Lindley	2
		Satyrium Swartz	90
		Satyridium Lindley	1
	Coryciinae Bentham	*Anochilus* Rolfe	3
		Pterygodium Swartz	13
		Corycium Swartz	15
		Ceratandra Lindley	3
		Evota Rolfe	3
		Disperis Swartz	50
Gastrodieae Lindley	Vanillinae Bentham	*Vanilla* Swartz	8
	Pogoniinae Pfitzer	*Nervilia* Gaudichaud	12
	Gastrodiinae Pfitzer	*Auxopus* Schlechter	2
		Didymoplexis Griffith	2
		Gastrodia R. Brown	2
Arethuseae Lindley	Bletiinae Bentham	*Ancistrochilus* Rolfe	2
		Calanthe R. Brown	1
		Phaius Loureiro	1
	Sobraliinae Schlechter	*Diceratostele* Summerhayes	1

Dendrobieae Endlicher	Bulbophyllinae Schlechter	*Bulbophyllum* Thouars	90
		Chaseëlla Summerhayes	1
		Cirrhopetalum Lindley	1
		Stolzia Schlechter	12
	Genyorchidinae Schlechter	*Genyorchis* Schlechter	6
Malaxideae Lindley		*Liparis* L.C. Richard	20
		Oberonia Lindley	1
		Malaxis Swartz	7
		Orestias Ridley	3
Vandeae Lindley	Sarcanthinae Bentham	*Acampe* Lindley	1
		Taeniophyllum Blume	1
	Angraecinae Summerhayes	*Angraecum* Bory	45
		Jumellea Schlechter	2
		Aeranthes Lindley	1
	Aerangidinae Summerhayes	*Listrostachys* Reichenbach *fil.*	1
		Microcoelia Lindley	12
		Encheiridion Summerhayes	2
		Chauliodon Summerhayes	1
		Taeniorrhiza Summerhayes	1
		Diaphananthe Schlechter	50
		Holmesia Cribb	1
		Podangis Schlechter	1
		Bolusiella Schlechter	6
		Chamaeangis Schlechter	7
		Plectrelminthus Rafinesque	1
		Aerangis Reichenbach *fil.*	26
		Barombia Schlechter	2
		Summerhayesia Cribb	2
		Rangaeris Summerhayes	6
		Ypsilopus Summerhayes	3
		Mystacidium Lindley	12
		Margelliantha Cribb	4
		Cyrtorchis Schlechter	16
		Solenangis Schlechter	2
		Dinklageella Mansfeld	2
		Eurychone Schlechter	2
		Calyptrochilum Kraenzlin	2
		Ancistrorhynchus Finet	13
		Sphyrarhynchus Mansfeld	1
		Triceratorhynchus Summerhayes	1
		Angraecopsis Kraenzlin	9
		Distylodon Summerhayes	1
		Eggelingia Summerhayes	2
		Tridactyle Schlechter	36
		Cardiochilos Cribb	1
		Nephrangis Summerhayes	1
		Rhaesteria Summerhayes	1
Polystachyeae Pfitzer		*Neobenthamia* Rolfe	1
		Polystachya Hooker	150
Cymbidieae Pfitzer	Cyrtopodiinae Bentham	*Acrolophia* Pfitzer	11
		Eulophia R. Brown	160
		Graphorkis Thouars	1
		Oeceoclades Lindley	12
		Pteroglossaspis Reichenbach *fil.*	3
	Cymbidiinae Bentham	*Ansellia* Lindley	2

CHAPTER ONE
The Habits of African Orchids

Orchid plants are always perennial and most of the different habits that their growth forms may exhibit are represented among the species that occur in Africa. The majority are herbaceous plants. About half of these grow in the ground, as do other terrestrial plants, their roots hidden from view, while the other half are epiphytes, with aerial roots that are attached to the bark of bushes and trees and more or less exposed to view.

A few terrestrials, including *Platylepis*, *Hetaeria* and *Cheirostylis*, have prostrate perennial stems, or rhizomes, that creep over the surface of the soil of forest or swamp, and root at the nodes into the soft substratum beneath. Every year a dormant bud on the rhizome produces a rosette of leaves. At the centre of the rosette a terminal inflorescence emerges, sometimes immediately, or, in other species, after a further period of growth and thickening of the rhizome has taken place below. Flowering and fruiting complete the growth of each stem and as the leaves collapse and die the rhizome, too, falls over, while a new bud on the prostrate part begins upward growth again.

Many terrestrial genera, particularly those in the tribe Orchideae, have a more pronounced dormant season that begins when the aerial parts of the plant die off and disappear after flowering and producing seeds. They have subterranean tubers, or fleshy rhizomes, from which growth begins anew each year when favourable conditions of temperature and moisture return. These terrestrial orchids produce solitary, upright flower-spikes, each of which arises from the apex of the most recently developed tuber. In *Disa* and *Satyrium*, the flowering stem is sometimes accompanied by a separate leafy shoot, but both are deciduous, disappearing after only a few months of life. In *Eulophia*, the underground fleshy rhizome produces two shoots every year, one leafy and one flowering, from two separated, sometimes quite distant, buds. In *Nervilia* there is a considerable interval between the appearance of the flowering shoot, which is precocious, and the emergence of the single conspicuous leaf that develops later from the lower, underground part of the stem.

Other terrestrial orchids have a tufted habit of growth and the leaves, lasting more than one season, though not for many, are referred to as 'evergreen'. The rosette of spotted leaves borne by *Stenoglottis* is occasionally evergreen and the enormous plicate leaves arising round the terrestrial pseudobulbs of *Calanthe* are always so.

Saprophytes are rare terrestrial plants, but in the warm and humid environment of the tropical forests this form of orchid life is occasionally encountered. The secret is that these pale brownish or pinkish plants, lacking leaves and completely devoid of chlorophyll, obtain their nourishment from fungi that can survive only in conditions that are continuously warm and damp. The fungus finds a home for some of its hyphae within the cells of the underground roots or tubers of the orchid. At the same time, other hyphae invade the tissues of decaying leaves and other vegetable and animal parts that litter the forest floor, to obtain nutrients which are subsequently shared with, or stolen by, the orchid plant. The genera *Epipogium*, *Didymoplexis*, *Gastrodia*, *Auxopus* and *Schwartzkopffia* have adopted completely this manner of living, and in the large genus *Eulophia* there are a few species that are able to survive in this way. They are usually referred to as saprophytes, because they are not green and obtain their nutrients from dead organic material, but it is the enzymes of the intermediate organism, the fungus, which actually carry out the decomposition process to release substances that the fungal hyphae, and subsequently the orchid, can absorb. These orchids could not live without their fungal partner and thus, in fact, are parasites upon the microscopic mycelium of the fungus which is truly the saprophyte.

The genus *Vanilla* is the only African orchid with a lianaceous habit of growth. The enormously long liana may be green and leafy, or reddish-coloured and completely leafless. It produces two kinds of roots with different structures and functions: one is very hairy, for absorbing water and nutrients from the soil, the other rather wiry and thin, for grabbing hold of passing vegetation to assist in its climb towards the light. Essentially terrestrial plants, the *Vanilla* vines often appear to be epiphytes, as they flower when the plants reach the light near the top of the forest canopy or in exposed positions on rocky cliffs.

Approximately half the orchids of Africa are epiphytes and the largest single group of them comprises the tribe Vandeae, whose members all display a monopodial habit of growth. The stem is usually leafy and grows continuously from its apical meristem, only branching occasionally. The inflorescences are borne laterally, in the axils of the leaves or just below them, and the roots, also, arise from the stem and are often extremely extensive, branching, and tangled. Many of these aerial roots contain abundant chloroplasts in their cortical regions, and presumably share the function of photosynthesis with the leaves. In the genera *Microcoelia, Encheiridion, Chauliodon, Taeniorrhiza, Taeniophyllum*, and some species of *Solenangis*, in which the leaves are reduced to brownish scales, the abundant roots fulfil this role entirely, as well as providing anchorage and absorbing mineral nutrients for the plants.

The other epiphytic orchids all exhibit a sympodial growth habit, in which a creeping rhizome remains more or less in contact with the surface of the substratum and from it one or more free stems arise every year. The growth of each free stem is limited and, when completed by producing an inflorescence from its base or apex, or sometimes, as in *Ansellia*, from intermediate nodes as well, this stem remains on the plant in a passive state; probably its stored nutrients provide energy for the new growth of the basal rhizome itself, or of another bud at one of its nodes, in the ensuing season. The free stems of some of these orchids are thin, as in *Oberonia*, but they bear fleshy, rather succulent leaves. In many genera, however, at least the lower part of the stem is swollen, sometimes tapering abruptly so that it is reminiscent of a bulb in shape. This kind of stem is called a pseudobulb; it may be formed of one or several nodes and is very variable in shape, round, ovoid, flattened or elongated like a cane. In *Bulbophyllum, Genyorchis* and *Chaseëlla*, the pseudobulbs are rather far apart on the basal rhizome, whereas in *Polystachya, Graphorkis, Liparis* and *Ansellia*, they are usually close together, giving the plant a tufted appearance. In both these types there is often regrowth from only one dormant bud every year, so that plants are formed in which the pseudobulbs are arranged in straight rows. Frequently, however, and always in certain species of *Stolzia, Bulbophyllum* and *Polystachya*, two or more buds develop simultaneously, so that a plant resembling a densely tufted mat of pseudobulbs is produced.

A number of epiphytes are not always restricted to trees and shrubs for a place to grow, and find almost bare rock surfaces an equally congenial site. Similarly, there are several terrestrial species that can adapt equally well to the shaded soil of the forest floor or to rock outcrops nearby. Some species of *Holothrix* and *Disperis* are terrestrials that can grow as lithophytes and, amongst the epiphytes, some *Rangaeris, Tridactyle, Aerangis, Bulbophyllum*, and *Polystachya* species may be found on rocks as well as trees. In a few genera there are species with an even wider ecological amplitude. Some *Stenoglottis, Brachycorythis, Cynorkis* and *Liparis* seem able to grow wherever there is space, and may be found on rocks, trees, or in the soil, wherever conditions have been favourable for germination and seedling establishment at some time in the past.

CHAPTER TWO

Details of the Orchid Plants

THE ROOTS

Anchorage and absorption are the primary functions of all orchid roots, and in many terrestrial species food storage and perennation are important too.

As in other monocotyledons, the vascular strand of an orchid root is confined to its centre and surrounded by many layers of cortical cells. In many orchids these, in turn, are protected from the environment by the velamen, a spongy covering of dead, air-filled cells, whose walls are held apart by irregular strands of thickening. The outer layer of this velamen is often modified to form many minute projections, similar to the absorptive root hairs that arise from the outer layer, the epidermis, of the underground roots of most flowering plants. Both aerial and underground roots of many orchids have developed a velamen layer, which, being filled with air when dry, imparts a greyish-white colour to them and a characteristic texture. Recent work has shown that the velamen is not only protective in function but also plays an important role in the absorption of nutrient-laden moisture and its retention, until it can be translocated into the living tissues of the plant via the central stele of the root.

In many aerial roots the cortical cells contain bright green chloroplasts and these add photosynthesis to the list of properties that orchid roots possess. This is particularly important for those plants that never bear green leaves, including species of *Microcoelia*, *Encheiridion* and other genera. There are several species in the genera *Mystacidium* and *Angraecopsis*, whose small plants normally bear leaves but may be temporarily leafless, in which the roots also appear bright green when the velamen is filled with water after rain.

Orchid roots are usually round in cross-section, but aerial roots often become flatten-ed and tape-like where they adhere to the host. In the well-named genus, *Taeniorrhiza*, and in *Sphyrarhynchus*, they always appear flat, as they also do in the large Asiatic genus, *Taeniophyllum*, which has one representative in Africa.

The position of the roots on the epiphytic orchids is varied. In the monopodial types, they may be fairly regularly arranged along the stem, as in *Diaphananthe* and many species of *Angraecum*, or they are restricted to the part of the stem below the leaves, as in *Podangis* and *Mystacidium*. In the epiphytes with a sympodial growth habit, the roots are produced at the base of the pseudobulbs or annual stems, and the intervening rhizome, whether long or short, is usually rootless. In the curious stems of the genus *Stolzia*, rooting may occur at any and every node, but in the somewhat similar, super-posed pseudobulbs of a section of the genus *Polystachya*, roots appear only at the base of each new growth.

Ansellia and *Graphorkis* are distinctive in bearing two kinds of roots: both kinds are white and branch extensively, but the penetrating, absorbing roots are much longer and thicker than the pointed, upright ones that surround the base of each plant. The function of these upright roots has not been investigated fully but it seems likely that they may form a trap, both a visible one for the ensnaring of insects, leaves and other debris whose subsequent disintegration and decomposition may make nutrients available, and a less noticeable one for the condensation and absorption of moisture in the form of dew — an important source of water in the seasonally dry habitats where these plants live.

The terrestrial species that undergo a period of dormancy have fleshy storage roots as well as slender, hairy, absorptive ones. Many of them also have one or more broad, fleshy tubers, which store both nutrients and water to maintain the life of the dormant bud during the dry season, and promote its development at the return of conditions favourable for growth.

In many parts of Africa these tubers and fleshy roots are used as sources of healing remedies, not just to ward off witchcraft or to ensure a happy outcome for a courting episode, but also to treat, apparently successfully, such diverse maladies as loss of speech, flatulence, worm infestations, difficulties in pregnancy, madness and many other real and imagined sorrows.

THE STEMS

The kind of stem an orchid plant develops determines its growth habit and the way in which it may be propagated. Upright stems bearing leaves and flowers are found in many terrestrial species and in the monopodial epiphytes, whereas in the sympodial epiphytes and some terrestrial species the stems are horizontal. These are referred to as rhizomes, which, in the terrestrial types, lie either above or below the surface of the soil.

In the forest-dwelling members of the subtribe Goodyerinae and in the genera *Malaxis* and *Orestias*, the slender stems persist as rhizomes for a number of years. They frequently branch, because more than one dormant bud on the rhizome develops an aerial flowering stem each year. This produces a rosette of leaves and a terminal raceme of flowers. Because of the horizontal nature of the rhizomes and their forward growth each year, a small population of these plants appears to advance across the forest floor and plants are not located in precisely the same spot in successive seasons.

In many species of *Eulophia*, *Acrolophia* and *Pteroglossaspis*, the rhizome is sub-terranean, and sometimes bears chains of swollen pseudobulbs along its length, each representing the annual increment at the base of a leafy shoot. These underground stems bear leaves, and a flowering stem or rachis, from separate nodes in both *Eulophia* and *Pteroglossaspis*. In *Acrolophia* only one shoot is produced on each short rhizome annually; densely leafy at first, this eventually produces an inflorescence at its apex.

The upright flower-spikes of terrestrial orchids in the tribe Orchideae are a familiar sight in many grassland areas of Africa. Clothed with bracts in their upper part, and usually embraced by enfolding leaves near the base, these stems develop very quickly, and are deciduous, disappearing as soon as flower, fruit and seed production have been completed.

In all the monopodial orchids the stem grows indefinitely, season after season. It bears leaves, of various shapes, in two distinct rows, and aerial roots and inflorescences in their axils, sometimes only after the leaf blade has fallen. The length of the stem determines the relative position of these organs and their spacing. In the genus *Angrae-cum* alone, the stem is a metre or more in length in some species and hardly developed at all in others.

Many monopodial orchids in Africa grow in an upright position. Often new branches arise from the base of a mature stem, which still continues to grow, so that a clump of upright stems eventually proves very conspicuous. When they become very elongated, as they often do in *Diaphananthe*, *Tridactyle*, and some *Cyrtorchis* species, these stems become heavier and eventually pendent, but often the growing tip of the plant still maintains an upright position. There are many smaller species in which the stem grows almost horizontally away from the host. Some of the species of *Aerangis*, and both species of *Eurychone*, all of which favour very shady forest habitats, grow in this way. Such stems hold the plant away from its host, assuring the leaves and flowers of ample space and fresh air. In two species in the genus *Ypsilopus*, the plants are always completely pendent. They hang below the lower surface of the branches of forest trees or parallel with their trunks.

Rhizomes, stems and pseudobulbs are sometimes difficult to distinguish in the remaining groups of epiphytic orchids. Sometimes the entire stem is swollen and pseudobulbous, as in *Stolzia* and the superposed species of *Polystachya*, where each new annual growth arises from a node near the apex of the last. Elongated stems of many nodes may arise close together from a short basal rhizome, as they do in other species of *Polystachya* and in *Ansellia*. Like *Bulbophyllum* and *Graphorkis*, the genus *Polystachya* has other species in which only one node, or just a few, are swollen to form a pseudobulb of many varied shapes — ovoid, globular, lens-shaped, conical or variously elongated — but each of these pseudobulbs represents an annual growth, arising from a basal, creeping and often branching rhizome. In the genera *Cirrhopetalum*, *Chaseëlla*, *Bulbophyllum* and *Genyorchis*, these annual growths are usually at some distance from each other and the branching rhizomes and roots form a network that completely encases the host branch or trunk. Old pseudobulbs become leafless and bare, or may remain partially covered in the papery, warty or hairy sheaths, which, at an earlier stage in their lives, surrounded the developing pseudobulb, sometimes as the basal part of a leaf. The surface of the pseudobulb itself is often dark green and shiny, but it may be paler, or a brilliant yellow or reddish colour, and it can be variously lined, furrowed, or channelled in a vertical or horizontal direction, and warty or rough, instead of smooth.

As in the monopodial types, a leaf is borne at each node of the sympodial stem, brown and scale-like on the rhizome, and green on the annual pseudobulb, but the position of the inflorescence varies. It is terminal in *Liparis*, *Stolzia* and *Polystachya*, and completes the apical growth of each pseudobulb, either early in its life or when it is fully mature, whereas in *Bulbophyllum* and *Cirrhopetalum* the inflorescence grows from the base of each pseudobulb. In the two last-named genera, several inflorescences are usually produced, and they may appear early in the growing season with the developing pseudobulb, or only after it has attained its full size, sometime during the following year.

THE LEAVES

As in other monocotyledons, an orchid leaf is divided into two parts: there is a basal sheath that clasps the stem, sometimes for a considerable distance, and may resemble the petiole or stalk of the broad leaves of trees and shrubs, and there is an expanded part, the lamina, which is enormously varied in its shape and size, thickness and venation. Often there is an articulation zone between the lamina and the sheath where the tissues break and the lamina falls off at the end of its useful life. The sheath is persistent, but turns brown or straw-coloured when it no longer supports the green lamina.

The number, position and arrangement of the leaves, and their texture, colour and longevity are related to the habit of the plants, the habitats in which they grow, and to the taxonomic position of the orchid species.

An orchid may have one or many leaves, or none at all. In many terrestrial species of the tribe Orchideae the leaves are either radical, forming a rosette around the base of the flowering stem, or paired, or single at the base of the plant, or they are cauline, borne along the stem, the largest near the base and the others decreasing in size upwards until they merge with the sheathing bracts and with the bracts that subtend the flowers. In some species of *Disa* and *Satyrium*, the leaves appear on a separate vegetative shoot, adjacent to the flower-spike. Their substance is succulent or fleshy, but they are mostly rather thin. They vary in shape from linear or almost grass-like, in some species of *Platycoryne*, *Herschelia*, *Disa* and *Habenaria*, to round and appressed to the ground in some species of the latter genus. *Bartholina* and *Holothrix* have similar prostrate leaves that are circular in outline but never very large or long-lived. In the forest-dwelling species of *Huttonaea*, *Habenaria* and *Cynorkis*, the leaves are larger and broader, while the largest leaves of all in this group are found in the grassland and forest-margin species of *Satyrium*. The leaves of all these species last no more than a single season, usually only a few months in duration.

Members of the tribes Neottieae, Cranichideae and Malaxideae are mostly terrestrial plants whose leaves are also short-lived but always broad and very thin. Often their venation forms a pattern, radiating from a point near the sheathing base, which is reflected by folds in the lamina and gives the leaf a pleated appearance. *Zeuxine*, *Malaxis* and *Liparis* have several species with plicate leaves. The genus *Nervilia*, in the tribe Gastrodieae, has the most spectacular leaf of all: round, elliptic or kidney-shaped in outline, the leaf appears singly, one to each plant, appressed to the ground or on a short erect petiole, so that with their plicate surface, proud, palmate venation and fluted margin, the leaves of a *Nervilia* population resemble miniature umbrellas set out to dry on the forest floor. The members of the tribe Arethuseae also bear plicate leaves, but these are long and lance-shaped, up to a metre in length in the terrestrial *Calanthe*, and a quarter of this size in the epiphytic *Ancistrochilus*.

In the epiphytic Dendrobieae the leaves are often modified for the storage or conservation of water. They are thick and leathery, last for many years, and are usually somewhat reduced in size. The smallest are found in *Chaseëlla*, which has six to ten needle-like leaves on top of each minute pseudobulb, while the genus *Bulbophyllum* can be readily subdivided according to whether each pseudobulb is surmounted by one leaf or two.

In the Polystachyeae the leaves are much more variable. They are narrow and grass-like along the slender stem of *Neobenthamia*, and also in some species of *Polystachya*. But this last genus is enormously varied in the possession, disposition and number of leaves per pseudobulb, as well as in their shape, size and coloration.

The leaves of the monopodial Vandeae are alternately arranged in two neat rows. In species where the internodes of the stem are very short, the leaves are crowded together and have closely overlapping bases. This provides the plant with the fan-shaped appearance displayed by *Bolusiella* and *Podangis*. In shape, the leaves are nearly always longer than broad; in many species they are parallel-sided, almost like a grass leaf, in others more or less elliptic. The leaf apex is nearly always conspicuously bilobed, and both the shape of the lobes and the size of the sinus between them are often of diagnostic value.

The short-stemmed, shade-loving, monopodial plants, such as many *Aerangis* and *Eurychone* species, have broader leaves that are much darker green in colour than those of the long-stemmed plants such as *Tridactyle* and *Calyptrochilum*. Plants of the latter genera grow in much stronger light, in the forest canopy, and their leaves are smaller, narrower and thicker. In a few species of *Tridactyle* and *Angraecum*, perhaps those which are exposed to the greatest extremes of temperature, the leaves are terete and only slightly channelled on the upper surface. Another unusual feature, in a few unrelated species, is the appearance of leaves in which the two halves of the upper surface have become fused together, producing a thick, fleshy leaf that appears flattened in a vertical plane instead of dorso-ventrally. In *Angraecum distichum*, leaves with this construction cover the slender curving branches very closely. Other genera with equitant leaves include *Podangis*, *Bolusiella* and *Rangaeris*.

Leafless orchids are members of this monopodial group, as mentioned earlier, and the saprophytic members of several different tribes also fail to develop leaves. A few species of *Vanilla* produce long, trailing, reddish stems, with plenty of roots but never a sign of a green leaf. The green *Vanilla* vines bear most attractive glossy leaves, each with a characteristic, acuminate apex.

In the huge genus *Eulophia* there are also some leafless plants, but the majority of species have leaves and within the genus there are many different kinds. They may be plicate and thin, or thick and fleshy, grass-like or sword-shaped, stiff or pliable, lasting a few short months or many years, and sometimes are somewhat variegated in colour.

Most orchid leaves are green, though they reveal many different shades of green — greyish, brown, reddish, yellowish or bluish — but a few, like *Holothrix orthoceras*, have a distinctly paler venation, while in several species of *Aerangis* and *Mystacidium* the venation provides a darker network across the lighter green leaf surface. *Stenoglottis fimbriata* is randomly spotted or barred with dark purplish-brown, and the leaves of *Manniella gustavii* are frequently splashed with silvery-grey spots.

Figure 1   African Orchid Plants I

1   Cheirostylis lepida: *terrestrial; an aerial rhizome, bearing few roots, that creeps over the surface of the soil; in its upper part several almost petiolate leaves clasp the stem and a dense terminal inflorescence completes the growth each year (redrawn from Summerhayes, 1968a x1/3).*

2   Satyrium longicauda: *terrestrial; an underground tuber supports the developing flowering shoot and a leafy shoot adjacent to it; by the end of the growing season the old tuber is wasted and thin, and a solid, fleshy, new one has formed below the pair of succulent leaves; both shoots develop many roots above the tubers (x1/8). Plant from Natal, South Africa.*

3   Schizochilus sulphureus: *terrestrial; a slender herb with a rounded tuber and numerous thickened roots; a few grass-like leaves are borne at the base of the annual stem, and the inflorescence is always nodding (redrawn from Summerhayes, 1968b, x1/2).*

4   Eulophia angolensis: *terrestrial; a thick, branching rhizome grows through soft, swampy soil, erecting an aerial leafy shoot that is accompanied by a separate flowering stem every summer; as soon as the leaves unfold new underground shoots arise from the base of the aerial shoots (x1/10). Plant from Natal, South Africa.*

5   Eulophia petersii: *terrestrial; the tough basal rhizome bears aerial pseudobulbs that are thick and succulent and have thick white roots at the base; each carries several sword-shaped leaves with serrated margins; the inflorescence, often 2–3 metres high, arises in spring with the newly forming pseudobulb (x1/6). Plant from Natal, South Africa.*

6.   Didymoplexis verrucosa: *terrestrial, saprophyte; a thick, pale, branching tuber with very few roots lies under the surface litter of the forest floor; leafless flowering shoots arise very quickly; the flowers are fugacious and the pedicels elongate tremendously in the fruiting stage (x1/5). Plant from Natal, South Africa.*

7   Vanilla polylepis: *terrestrial; a long, climbing stem ascends trees, branches, rocks and cliffs to a height of several metres; the dark, glossy leaves arise above or opposite a root and the inflorescences are borne at the tip of lateral branches (x1/8). Plant from Kenya.*

8   Rangaeris amaniensis: *epiphyte or lithophyte; mature plants bear long, straggling stems with many thickened roots and two rows of leathery leaves near the upturned tip; the few-flowered inflorescences arise in the axils of the leaves (x1/4). Plant from Kenya.*

9   Aerangis verdickii: *epiphyte or lithophyte; a tough succulent plant with a fan of large fleshy leaves; thick white roots and long inflorescences arise near the base of the stem (x1/3). Plant from Transvaal, South Africa.*

10   Bulbophyllum scaberulum: *epiphyte or lithophyte; an elongated woody rhizome bears a four-angled pseudobulb at the tip of each year's growth; two leathery leaves arise from the apex of the pseudobulb, and the curious inflorescence is produced from its base after a long resting season (x1/4). Plant from Transkei.*

11   Oberonia disticha: *epiphyte; long, slender stems bear two rows of closely overlapping equitant leaves and a terminal inflorescence of tiny flowers; the stems are often pendent and are attached to the substratum by narrow, wiry roots (x1/3). Plant from Transvaal, South Africa.*

12   Polystachya albescens: *epiphyte; long, narrow, cane-like pseudobulbs arise close together on a branching basal rhizome; each bears several grass-like leaves and a much-branched, terminal inflorescence (x1/7). Plant from Natal, South Africa.*

All the illustrations in these figures have been made from living plants in the author's collection, except where another source is indicated.

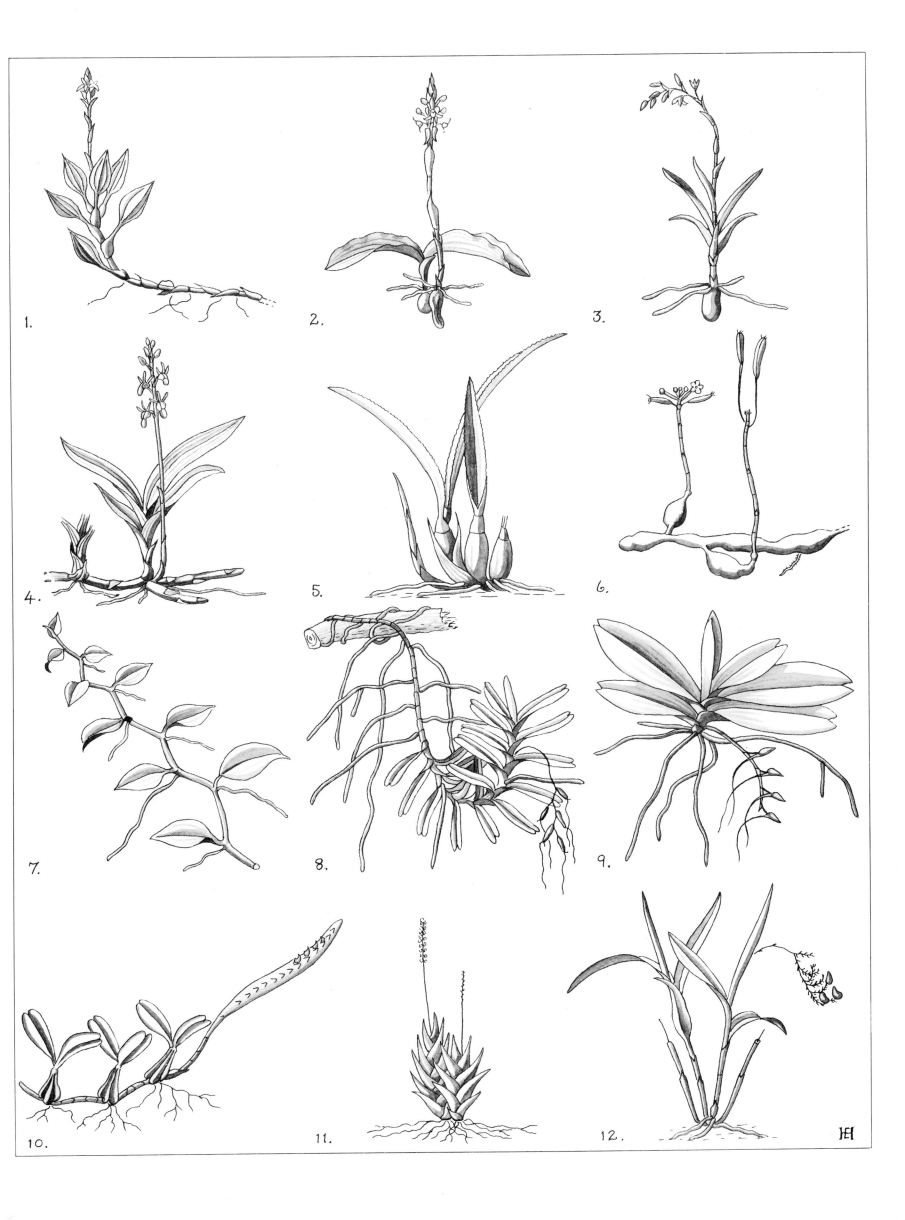

1.

2.

3.

4.

5.

6.

7.

8.

9.

10.

11.

12.

HH

Figure 2   *African Orchid Plants II*

1   Platylepis glandulosa: *terrestrial; an aerial rhizome that creeps over the surface of the soil and bears few penetrating roots; several broad leaves and a terminal inflorescence complete its growth each year (x1/4). Plant from Natal, South Africa.*

2   Eulophia foliosa: *terrestrial; a horizontal, underground rhizome that is described as moniliform, that is, each annual growth, or pseudobulb, resembling a bead on a string; a tuft of plicate leaves and a separate flowering stem arise from the new pseudobulb each spring (x1/6). Plant from Natal, South Africa.*

3   Brachycorythis ovata: *terrestrial; an upright, leafy stem that bears a terminal inflorescence (x1/5). Plant from Natal, South Africa.*

4   Disa uniflora: *terrestrial; axillary shoots arise underground and grow out at the sides of the upright parent plant, producing a clump of many stems bearing long linear leaves; each shoot eventually terminates in a few-flowered inflorescence (x1/5). Plant from Cape Province.*

5   Eulophia quartiniana: *terrestrial; a pseudobulb of several nodes develops above the soil surface within the base of the leaves of each annual shoot; the flowering stem arises at the same time as the leaves, but from a separate bud at the base of the last-formed pseudobulb (x1/6). Plant from Ethiopia.*

6   Liparis bowkeri: *terrestrial or epiphyte; the new pseudobulb develops from the base of the previous year's growth, and bears a short terminal inflorescence while its leaves and pseudobulb are still in the early stages of expansion (x1/3). Plant from Natal, South Africa.*

7   Stolzia repens: *epiphyte or lithophyte; the rhizomatous stem creeps over the surface of the substratum and forms indistinct pseudobulbs, each with two leaves at its apex and a single terminal flower; new pseudobulbs arise just below the apex of the previous one, and branching occurs frequently (redrawn from Piers, 1968, x1).*

8   Polystachya cultriformis: *epiphyte; the basal rhizome is short and compact; each pseudobulb that arises from it is encased in sheaths and consists of only one swollen internode; it bears a single leaf and an apical inflorescence (x1/3). Plant from Kenya.*

9   Polystachya vaginata: *epiphyte or lithophyte; each pseudobulb arises near the base of the growth that precedes it; it consists of several nodes, and bears several narrow leaves as well as a terminal inflorescence (x1/3). Plant from Kenya.*

10   Polystachya vulcanica: *epiphyte; each pseudobulb arises a little distance above the base of the preceding one; it bears a single fleshy leaf and a short, terminal inflorescence above the stick-like pseudobulb (x1/3). Plant from Uganda.*

11   Cyrtorchis praetermissa: *epiphyte; a tough stem with upright, monopodial growth; the stem bears leaves in two regular rows in the terminal part, inflorescences in the axils of the lowermost ones, and aerial roots from the older part (x1/3). Plant from Natal, South Africa.*

12   Angraecopsis amaniensis: *epiphyte; a very abbreviated stem with a small fan of leaves and radiating roots at its base; pendent inflorescences are borne below the leaves (x1). Plant from Kenya.*

13   Eurychone rothschildiana: *epiphyte; an elongated stem with a fan of two to five broad leaves in its apical part; the stems are pendent from branches or lianas, or they stand away from the supporting host in a horizontal direction; the few-flowered inflorescences arise below the leaves (x1/4). Plant from Uganda.*

14   Ypsilopus longifolius: *epiphyte; the monopodial stem is always pendent and bears a stiff fan of grass-like leaves near its apex; the few-flowered inflorescences arise below the leaves and are also pendent (x1/3). Plant from Kenya.*

15   Diaphananthe xanthopollinia: *epiphyte; an untidy, straggling plant with long, branched stems that are usually pendent, but grow upwards at their tips; many long roots and short inflorescences are borne below the leaves (x1/4). Plant from Natal, South Africa.*

16   Bolusiella iridifolia: *epiphyte; a short stem bears a fan of closely overlapping, succulent leaves and a few narrow roots at its base; the inflorescences arise in the axils of the lowermost leaves (x1). Plant from Kenya.*

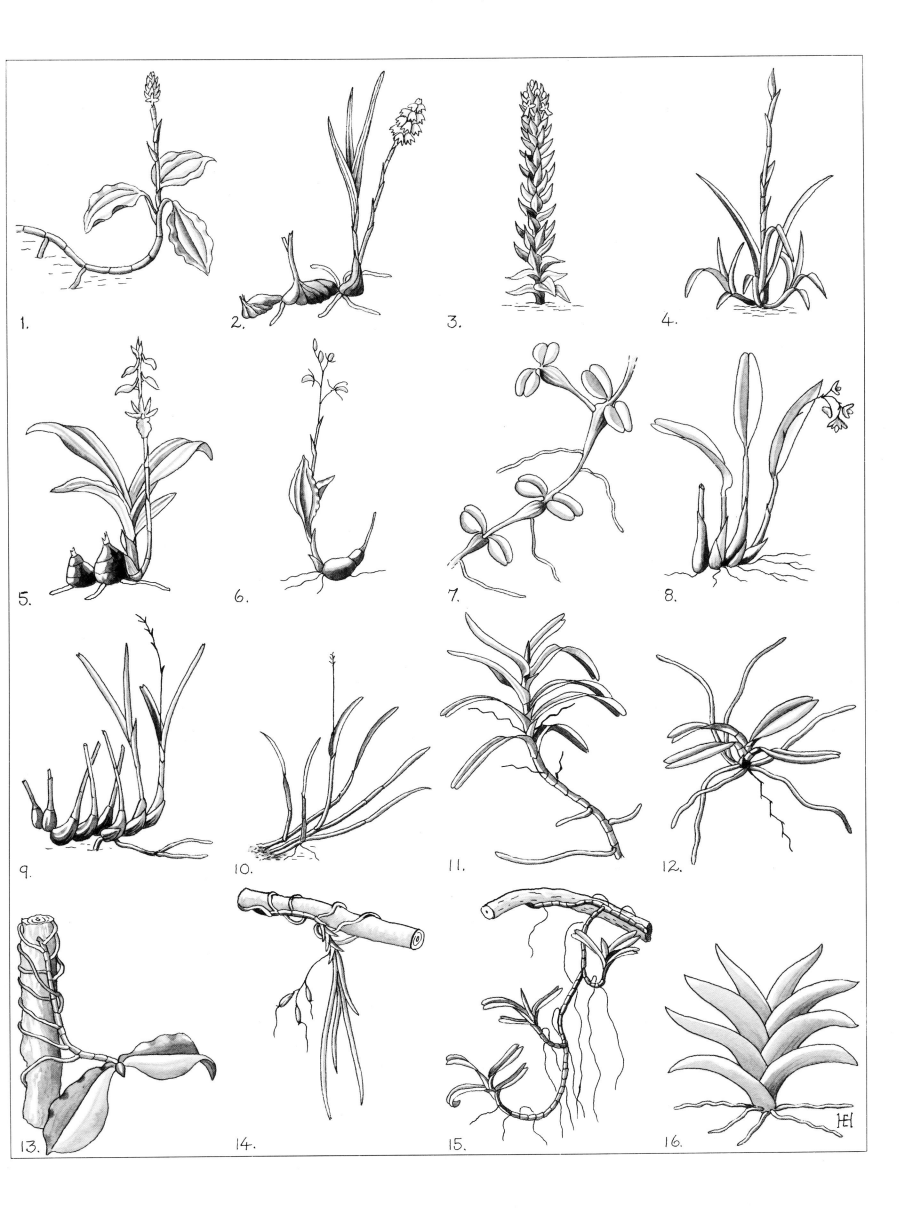

1.

2.

3.

4.

5.

6.

7.

8.

9.

10.

11.

12.

13.

14.

15.

16.

Figure 3   *African Orchid Plants III*

1   Cynorkis kassnerana: *terrestrial, or rarely epiphyte; several tubers buried in moss carry the plant through the cooler and drier part of the year; with the onset of rain and warmer weather a single large leaf is produced with the flowering shoot in its axil; hairy roots spread out from the base of the shoot into the surrounding substratum (x1). Plant from Kenya.*

2   Satyrium parviflorum: *terrestrial; one elongated tuber overwinters in dry soil and produces a leafy shoot in late spring; a pair of enormous leaves is produced before the flowering shoot elongates and almost immediately a new tuber begins to form at their base (x1/5). Plant from Natal, South Africa.*

3   Stenoglottis woodii: *terrestrial or lithophyte; a rosette of leaves arises every spring above the elongated tuberous roots; fine, feeding roots spread out from the base of the short stem which bears a terminal inflorescence in midsummer (x1/6). Plant from Natal, South Africa.*

4   Huttonaea fimbriata: *terrestrial; a shade-loving forest species that grows in summer from a single ovoid tuber; the flowering stem arises through the sheath of a large, petiolate, cordate leaf; new tubers are formed at the end of white roots that penetrate the litter of the forest floor (x1/3). Plant from Natal, South Africa.*

5   Disperis lindleyana: *terrestrial; another species of the forest floor that grows swiftly and flowers in late spring from an ellipsoid underground tuber; after fruiting, a new tuber forms at the base of the stem to carry the plant through the dormant period; seedling plants bear only a single heart-shaped leaf for several years until the underground tuber produced below them has reached a certain size (x1/5). Plant from Natal, South Africa.*

6   Calanthe sylvatica: *terrestrial; a plant of shady streamsides, characterised by its enormous plicate leaves with small pseudobulbs within their bases and a terminal inflorescence (x1/8). Plant from Natal, South Africa.*

7   Angraecum subulatum: *epiphyte; a tiny, slender epiphyte with terete, almost wiry leaves, with subulate tips and tiny inflorescences borne laterally on the stems (x1). Leaf section x3. Plant from Nigeria.*

8   Nervilia adolphii: *terrestrial; a plant of the woodlands of west and central Africa, with single-flowered inflorescences appearing before the dark green prostrate, shortly petiolate leaves (x1, drawn from Stolz 1870, the type specimen from Tanzania, preserved at Natal University).*

9   Chaseëlla pseudohydra: *epiphyte; a minute plant with rows of tiny pseudobulbs distantly arranged on a wiry rhizome; each ovoid pseudobulb carries six to ten needle-like leaves at its apex and a single-flowered inflorescence from its base (x1, drawn from Stewart 1194, collected in Kenya).*

10   Angraecum distichum: *epiphyte; a tufted plant of many branching stems with stiff, succulent leaves that are narrowly triangular in cross-section; solitary flowers are borne on short peduncles in the axils of the leaves (x1). Plant from Liberia.*

11   Microcoelia obovata: *epiphyte; a leafless orchid with a short stem bearing brownish scales and many thick, greyish roots of varying length; a few inflorescences are borne among the roots every year (x1/2). Plant from Kenya.*

12   Graphorkis lurida: *epiphyte; conspicuous swollen pseudobulbs, each composed of several nodes, are surrounded at the base by thick, penetrating roots and more slender upright roots; the paniculate inflorescence arises from the base of the mature leafless pseudobulb before the new leaves are produced (x1). Plant from Uganda.*

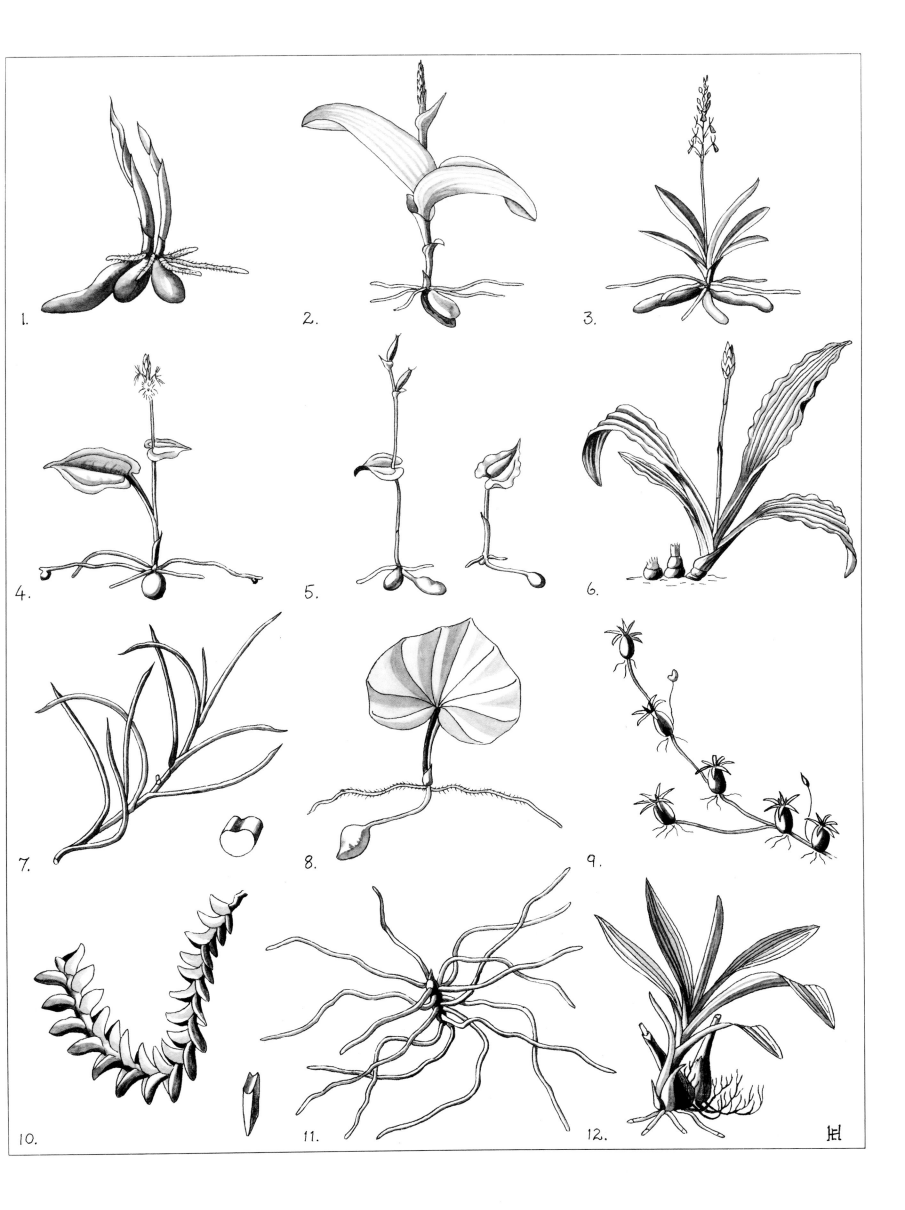

1.

2.

3.

4.

5.

6.

7.

8.

9.

10.

11.

12.

Details of the Flowers

ARRANGEMENT

Orchid flowers may be arranged on the plant in five different ways, as a simple spike, raceme or umbel, occasionally solitary and sometimes in a branching panicle, and these are described in detail below. There is usually a bract, a structure resembling a miniature leaf, at the point on the axis of the inflorescence where the pedicel of each flower is inserted. Below the flowers, the inflorescence is often ensheathed by larger bracts that do not support flowers, and this sterile portion of the inflorescence stalk is referred to as the peduncle.

Orchid inflorescences are commonly known as spikes although very few correctly merit this term, which implies that each flower is sessile, that is, inserted without a stalk, on the rachis. In *Chamaeangis*, *Tridactyle*, *Bolusiella* and many species of *Bulbophyllum*, the flowers may look as if they have no stalk but in fact there is a short strip of sterile tissue between the inferior ovary and the rachis.

The most common form of inflorescence among the African orchids is the raceme. A number of flowers are borne along a single, unbranched rachis. Usually they open in succession from the base upwards. Each flower has a distinct pedicel, quite separate from the inferior ovary below the perianth, although it may not be easily distinguished from it until the ovary enlarges to form a fruit. In most racemes the flower-bearing rachis is much longer than the peduncle, but in many species of *Angraecopsis*, and some species of *Bulbophyllum*, the peduncle is the longer. Usually the inflorescence stalk is green or brown, and round in cross-section. Occasionally it is swollen in the flower-bearing portion, as in some *Chamaeangis* and *Bulbophyllum* species, or it may be four-sided, as in some species of *Tridactyle* and *Rangaeris*, or flattened, with wing-like outgrowths on two sides, as it is in one whole section of the genus *Bulbophyllum*. The flowers are usually arranged around the inflorescence rather regularly: either spirally, as in most of the terrestrial species and some of the epiphytes; or in two formal rows on either side of the rachis, as they are in most of the Vandeae. In a few species of the latter tribe, in the genera *Chamaeangis* and *Diaphananthe*, they are arranged in whorls of three or five along the rachis. In several *Holothrix* and *Bulbophyllum* species, although neatly arranged in two rows, the flowers are twisted to face one direction, so that a one-sided, or secund, inflorescence is produced.

The rachis may be long, bearing well-spaced flowers, or it may be very abbreviated so that the flowers appear clustered together in tight heads. In several species of *Ancistrorhynchus* the peduncle is almost absent, and a dense, spherical mass of flowers, held close to the stem, is the result. The inflorescence is also very short in *Podangis*, but here the flowers have long pedicels, so that they are individually well displayed, away from the base of the plant.

The longest racemes are found in several terrestrial plants: *Epipactis africana* may bear only a few dozen flowers but they are widely spaced so that the raceme is a metre long, or more; in the South African *Corycium magnum*, the flowers are arranged in a close spiral over a metre or so and hundreds may be present in a single inflorescence. Several species of *Disa* and *Satyrium* are also remarkable for the number of flowers they carry on their racemes or spikes. The flowers may open almost simultaneously, producing a spike that resembles a glowing, golden candle in *Disa ochrostachya* and *D. woodii*, or sometimes they open in spasmodic sequence, presenting a concentric target of blooms and buds in *Acampe* and *Ceratandra*. By their aggregation, these small blooms produce an effect that is at once attractive, eye-catching and distinctively orchidaceous.

Cirrhopetalum is the only genus in which the flowers are arranged in an umbel, with their pedicels all radiating from one point at the tip of the peduncle. In two species of *Malaxis*, the flowers arise so closely on the short rachis that they present the appearance of an umbel, but this is false: it is only an abbreviated raceme, and most of the species in the genus bear their flowers in an elongated raceme or spike.

In the epiphytic genus *Jumellea* and the terrestrial *Bartholina*, the inflorescence bears only a single flower. This habit is sometimes followed in other genera too, notably *Angraecum, Brownleea, Nervilia* and *Stolzia*, but they also contain some species that normally have multiflowered inflorescences.

Ansellia and *Graphorkis* are prolific and produce many flowers in branching panicles. In some species of *Oeceoclades, Polystachya* and *Eulophia*, a panicle is also produced, and in the widespread but rarely seen genus, *Corymborkis*, the inflorescence is sometimes paniculate.

The position of an inflorescence on the stem, whether it is produced terminally, or carried laterally, in the axil of a leaf, has often been used as a character of taxonomic importance, both for the differentiation of genera and at higher levels of classification. Newcomers to Africa soon learn to distinguish the genus *Polystachya*, which bears its inflorescence at the apex of its pseudobulbs, from the somewhat similar genera *Genyorchis* and *Bulbophyllum*, where several inflorescences arise from below the base of each pseudobulb.

In all the monopodial orchids, the inflorescences are borne in lateral positions on the stem, either below the leaves or in the leaf axils. Many of these genera are extremely floriferous. In good growing conditions, in nature or in cultivation, very large numbers of flowers are produced. Tiny plants may be covered in blossoms on ten or a dozen racemes, while older plants, with many stems, present a closely packed bouquet of flowers. Even species of *Jumellea*, which bear only one flower in each inflorescence, and some species of *Angraecum*, which bear very few, may be covered with hundreds of blooms if the plants are large enough.

COLOUR

African orchids have the reputation of being either white or dull in colour, but this is an over-simplification that the later pages of this book will prove is patently untrue. Dazzling white is especially prized, particularly when its purity is combined with an elegant shape and a delicate nocturnal fragrance. In many white flowers the surface is enlivened by an exciting texture: it may resemble polished ivory in colour and smoothness; it may be matt, like candle wax; or it may look bright and crystalline as light scintillates on the rounded surfaces of its cells. Some white flowers present variations in colour with time: there are species of both *Rangaeris* and *Cyrtorchis* in which the greenish buds fade to form pure white flowers that age to apricot and orange before they collapse two or three weeks later, or sooner if pollinated.

White flowers are frequent among the African orchids, particularly among the monopodial, epiphytic species, but also among the terrestrials. Both groups demonstrate, however, that there are many shades of white, and that its purity is frequently polluted by shades of pink, grey, green and brown. But brilliant primary colours are present, too. These are vivid and striking, whether painting the perianth in pure tones or contrasting mixtures. Often the colours of the spectrum are themselves mixed so that all the varied hues, tints, shades and tones of the colour chart are represented. Thus, not only white but a complete rainbow of colours can be traced amongst the flowers of African orchids.

Violet, indigo and blue are found in the terrestrial genera *Herschelia*, *Disa* and *Brownleea*, and are mixed with red pigments to form purple and lilac in *Calanthe*, *Disa*, *Cynorkis*, and *Stenoglottis*. Many species of *Habenaria* and *Bonatea* are predominantly green, as are the flowers of *Corycium*, *Pterygodium*, *Roeperocharis*, *Centrostigma* and many others. But the greens merge with yellow or brown, and contrasting white parts are also often present in some part of the perianth. Yellow is a very common colour among African orchid species. It is frequent in *Polystachya*, and is the basic colour of *Acampe* and *Ansellia*, while in the terrestrial species there are some brilliant yellow spikes of *Disa* and racemes of *Eulophia*. Orange is the keynote of *Platycoryne*, and appears occasionally in the large genera *Eulophia*, *Disa* and *Satyrium*. Reds of a rich and vibrant brilliancy are present, too, in the famous *Disa uniflora*, as well as in other striking members of this genus, and in the rare and rarely seen *Polystachya kermesina*. Pinks and browns and other derivations of red are very common colours in many genera of terrestrial orchids, and in *Bulbophyllum*, *Polystachya* and several other epiphytes. Dark brown and almost black are as attractive in several species of *Corycium* as many brighter colours in other genera.

Many flowers have different colours in different parts of the perianth: there are green or bronze sepals and petals in *Plectrelminthus* and *Angraecum eburneum*, with a large white lip, and in *Habenaria* very often there are a green lip and sepals, but white petals or white stigma lobes; the striking *Aerangis luteo-alba* var. *rhodosticta* contrasts its creamy-yellow perianth with a bright red column, and in the bluish-lilac hood of many *Herschelia* flowers, tiny petals of a brilliant green catch the eye.

Spots, bars, stripes and patches of toning and contrasting colours are common and varied. Often they are present on a miniature scale and the flowers invite close examination for a full perception of their pattern, intricacy and importance. For there is nearly always an overall design of these embellishments that leads the eye of the observer, or the insect, to the very centre of the flower, to the base of the column or the site of the stigmatic surface which is waiting to receive the pollen whose arrival must precede fertilisation and seed formation. Orchid flowers are coloured and decorated for a purpose, for the attraction, enticement or deception of an insect — a fly, bee, moth or butterfly — which alone can perform this vital act of transfer for them.

FRAGRANCE AND LONGEVITY

An attractive appearance is not the only asset that orchids flaunt as a pollinator-attracting device. Fragrance is just as important, sometimes more so, and often it is a combination of odour and looks that attracts the desired visitor.

Many of the smallest flowers have an especially strong scent, perhaps to compensate for their lack of attractive surface area. Conversely the larger, more brightly coloured flowers, are often scentless, at least to humans, but these are animals endowed with a relatively poor sense of smell and a very restricted vocabulary for describing the scents they can perceive.

There is no typical orchid perfume. Instead, orchid flowers are described as scented like roses, violets, gardenias, tuberoses, carnations, bananas or cloves. The smell is said to be sweet or seductive, fresh or fleeting, heavy or intoxicating, depending, perhaps, on the time of day, the number of flowers present, and the perspicacity of the observer. In those orchid flowers whose fragrances have been analysed, the chemicals responsible for the pleasant smell have been identified as various different terpenes, rather common components of the essential oils responsible for the fragrance of roses, gardenias and other flowers with which orchids are often compared. It is the proportions of the various substances present which determine the slight differences in perfume that are noticeable in different species in a particular genus and are responsible for the differences between genera.

Perfume production is not usually a continuous process. In the brightly coloured orchids it is most noticeable during the day, when rising temperatures and sunny conditions promote the release of essential oils from the flower surface. Bees and butterflies are also active under these conditions. White and pale-flowered orchids are rarely or only slightly scented in the daytime. As dusk falls *Aerangis*, *Rangaeris* and others begin to produce a most penetrating perfume, which continues throughout the evening hours and combines with their pale colour to lure nocturnal insects to pollinating activities in return for ambrosial refreshment.

A few orchids produce odours which humans describe as unpleasant, but the small flies that are attracted to smells of carrion in various stages of decay are ideally suited in size and shape to creep over the delicately hinged lip of *Bulbophyllum* and *Cirrhopetalum* flowers and perform the act of pollination for them. The smell released by flowers of *Cirrhopetalum umbellatum* has been described as resembling that of decaying fish, as also has that of the terrestrial, plum-coloured blooms of *Malaxis maclaudii*.

Colour is attractive and fragrance effective for varying periods in the life of an orchid flower: both fade soon after pollination has occurred. In anticipation of the event, the duration of flowers is varied. Some delicate blooms are more long-lasting than others that appear much tougher. Those which develop rapidly, like *Didymoplexis*, last only a few hours, while those that mature more slowly may survive for a month in great beauty. Slugs and other predatory grazers sometimes bring to a close the life of a still-unpollinated flower of *Ansellia* or *Eulophia* after more than several weeks of waiting.

SIZE AND SHAPE

Whilst there is great variety in size among the African orchids, the only record for which some of them might compete on a world basis is that for the smallest. The flowers of *Oberonia disticha* and *Microcoelia exilis* are only a millimetre or two in diameter, and there are several species of *Bulbophyllum*, as well as *Genyorchis*, *Chaseëlla*, *Angraecum* and *Rhaesteria*, whose flowers are not much bigger. The largest flowers in this continent are found in some of the tropical species of *Angraecum*, and the longest spurs, 15–25 cm in length, in *Plectrelminthus* and *Aerangis*.

The statistics of African orchid flowers, measured in length or diameter, are not particularly striking, but it is primarily shape, not size, that determines aesthetic appeal. The silhouettes and shapes of these flowers are always pleasingly symmetrical and very attractive. Individually, each flower may delimit a circle or star, triangle or hexagon, oblong or oval. Each has its charm, and whether its shape is demure, dainty, elegant or bizarre, it brings delectation to the careful observer, and promises a reward of some kind to the observant insect.

STRUCTURE

In the field there is always a certain charisma about an orchid plant in flower. Somehow it seems rather special: it stands up, proudly proclaiming its personality, even before the finder takes a quick look at its structure to confirm its identity. Several features of an orchid flower make it absolutely unmistakable.

Like those of the iris family, orchid flowers have three petaloid sepals and three petals perched above an inferior ovary, which is often not fully developed by the time the flowers open. The flowers are bilaterally symmetrical and for convenience the sepals are distinguished as an intermediate, odd, or dorsal one, and a pair of laterals. Often the intermediate sepal is different in size or shape from the lateral pair. Similarly, two of the petals resemble each other, and the third member of this whorl is highly modified to form the lip, or labellum. In the centre of the flower the single stamen of the African orchids is united with the stigma in a relatively massive structure, the gynostemium, or column, which stands upright above the base of the lip or projects forward above it. The lip and the column are the most specialised parts of the orchid flower; they are the features that demonstrate its distinctiveness and indicate its identity, however much the other parts may be modified.

A common phenomenon of orchid flowers is the twisting of the ovary or pedicel through 180°. The twist takes place in the mature flower bud, just before the flowers open. Thus many orchid flowers are resupinate, with the lip presented in the lowermost position. There are relatively few in which no twisting has occurred and whose flowers are described as non-resupinate. *Polystachya* and *Satyrium* are conspicuous African genera in which the lip is uppermost and the ovary untwisted. In *Plectrelminthus* and some species of *Angraecum* further twisting has occurred so that the lip is uppermost and the ovary twisted and curled through a complete circle or two.

SEPALS

In most orchids the sepals are similar and free from each other. They spread at an angle of 120°, forming a basic framework for the flower.

In some genera the dorsal sepal is very different in shape from the laterals, forming a distinct hood or helmet at the apex of the flower. In *Disa, Herschelia, Brownleea, Schizodium* and *Monadenia*, this hood bears a tubular extension, the spur, which may be upright, horizontal or pendent, and whose inner surface is nectariferous. Other terrestrial genera, including *Bonatea, Habenaria, Centrostigma* and *Disperis*, also have dorsal sepals that are hooded, saccate, or even spurred in a few members of the latter genus, and in these genera the hood is accentuated by the petals, or one of their lobes, being more or less attached to its front margins. In several species of *Bulbophyllum*, the dorsal sepal is enlarged and inflated: its tissues appear thick and are more brightly coloured than the rest of the flower; while in others the dorsal sepal is hairy, or ciliate, around its margin, over its whole surface, or at its tip.

In *Polystachya*, the two lateral sepals are uppermost in the flower and are united along their inner margin to an extension of the column foot to form a distinctive mentum, or chin. A similar mentum is formed by the lateral sepals, on the lower side of the flower, in *Bulbophyllum*, *Stolzia* and *Genyorchis*. In *Cirrhopetalum*, these sepals twist over beyond the mentum, and their outer margins meet and fuse centrally, forming a platform with their outer surface uppermost. The lateral sepals in *Disperis* are often united towards the base and each is further remarkable in the possession of a spur or sac about halfway along its length. In *Liparis* and *Malaxis*, the briefly united lateral sepals stand behind the lip, making that segment appear almost double.

In *Cheirostylis* and *Manniella*, the sepals are united to one another and to the petals for part of their length, as they are also in the saprophytic genera *Auxopus* and *Didymoplexis* and in the leafless, epiphytic genus *Taeniophyllum*. In the terrestrial genus *Satyrium* there is union between all the perianth parts. In all these genera the flower is thus tubular at its base.

PETALS

The paired petals of African orchid flowers are immensely varied in shape, size and colour and are often quite different from the sepals in each of these features. In several genera they are small, not necessarily insignificant but forming a less conspicuous part of the flower than the sepals. In *Disa* and its allies, although often two-lobed and brightly coloured, they are tucked inside the dominant dorsal sepal. In *Disperis* and *Platycoryne*, they are attached to the margins of the dorsal sepal and often rather narrow, while in *Bulbophyllum* and *Genyorchis* they may be very small indeed.

In *Eulophia*, they are usually very conspicuous, whether similar to the sepals or very much larger and brighter. The larger petals are often flushed or veined in a darker colour on their inner surface, almost as if they are suffused with blushes as they fall coyly forward to conceal the column.

Throughout the Vandeae the sepals and petals are rather similar to each other, giving a somewhat 'star-like' appearance to many of the flowers. *Rangaeris*, *Cyrtorchis*, *Aerangis*, *Ypsilopus* and *Mystacidium* species are often described as starry since the lip is also very similar to the other perianth parts.

The clawed, lobed and fimbriate petals of *Huttonaea* are the most extraordinary in the Orchideae, and the lobed petals of *Holothrix*, although tiny, also present a whiskery outline to the face of the flowers. In the large genus *Habenaria* any extravagance is possible: the petals may be entire or two-lobed; if the latter, the upper, posterior lobe is often more or less attached to the edge of the dorsal sepal, while the lower, anterior lobe is extremely varied in shape and size, sometimes resembling the outer lobes of the lip, in other species papillose, or hairy, and in others erect and horn-like.

THE LIP

The lip of the orchid flower provides a landing-place for insect visitors, a colourful flag to attract them, a source of food in its surface callosities, or a pleasant drink from the nectar in the spur at its base. It is the most highly modified tepal of the flower and is often its most conspicuous feature. Very rarely, it is so reduced, as in *Brownleea*, as to be almost absent. Sometimes it is very complex, but tucked inside the other perianth parts partially concealing the column, as in *Disperis* and *Corycium*, and thus rather difficult to distinguish.

Most orchid flowers bear a lip that is larger than the rest of the flower and either simple in shape or three-lobed. The simple shapes are very varied, from small and tongue-like in many *Disa* species, to round or shell-shaped in some species of *Angraecum*, or deeply funnel-shaped as in *Microcoelia* and *Eurychone*. They may be flat, concave, or twisted, and many bear a tubular extension at the base which is a nectariferous spur. This is very varied in length and shape, from only a single millimetre in diameter and completely globular in *Microcoelia exilis*, to 20 cm long and corkscrew-twisted in *Aerangis kotschyana*. *Satyrium* is unique among the African orchids in bearing two spurs, one on each side of the base of its lip. The margin of these simple lips may be entire, hairy, or finely divided into many narrow lobes that form a fringe as in *Huttonaea*, *Bartholina* and some species of *Holothrix* and *Herschelia*.

For descriptive purposes it is often convenient to distinguish the basal part of the lip, the hypochile, which may be articulated where it is attached to the base of the column or very constricted and narrow when it is called the claw, from the middle part, the mesochile, and the apical part, the epichile. Each part may be variously lobed at its margin and may support outgrowths of diverse shapes and sizes on its surface.

In many genera, the lip is three-lobed in its basal part, as it is in *Ansellia*, *Ancistrochilus*, *Bolusiella* and some species of *Eulophia*. In *Calanthe*, the two side lobes arise from the mesochile, the hypochile being claw-like and fused to the lower surface of the column. In *Habenaria* and *Bonatea*, there is also a basal claw before the narrow or fimbriated side lobes diverge from the midlobe of the lip. In *Tridactyle*, it is the apical part that is three-lobed; often the side lobes are fringed and there is a pair of auricles on either side of the lip base.

The lateral lobes of the lip may be erect, sheltering the surface of the midlobe, the disc, between them and the forward projecting column, or they may spread out away from the flower, enlarging the receptive surface of the lip. In *Brachycorythis*, there are upright side lobes on the hypochile of most species and variations in the spreading side lobes of the mesochile or epichile as well. In *Polystachya*, only two lateral lobes are usually present, but they may arise from the base, middle, or apex of the lip.

The middle lobe of the three-lobed lip is usually different from the side lobes, sometimes larger, but frequently smaller. In *Calanthe* and *Oeceoclades*, it is itself divided into two rounded lobes, so that the complete lip appears four-lobed.

Many of these complex lips also bear a spur at their base. Spurs of various shapes and sizes are found throughout the Vandeae, in most of the Orchidinae, and many of the Cyrtopodiinae. Here and there the occasional species lacks a spur on the lip: it is absent from *Ansellia*, some of the Disinae and Coryciinae; but on the whole the calcarate condition can be regarded as characteristic of many African orchids.

In *Phaius* and *Vanilla*, the lip is indistinctly three-lobed and trumpet-shaped, completely enfolding the column, and with a waxy, crispate margin.

The lip is usually attached to the rest of the orchid flower below the column, or sometimes to the downward extension of the column, its foot. In the latter event, the lip is often extremely mobile, as it is in *Bulbophyllum* and *Cirrhopetalum*, the articulation with the column foot forming a delicately balanced hinge. Other lips are usually immovable, and may actually be fused to the base of the column in *Calanthe, Platylepis* and some species of *Eulophia*, or to the other perianth parts, as in *Satyrium* and *Manniella*, so that a tubular flower is formed.

The lip is often the most colourful part of the flower, being differently coloured, or more densely marked with spots or bars than the rest of the perianth.

In addition to its striking coloration it is frequently decorated with unusual outgrowths called keels, calli, crests, lamellae and appendages. Some of these are also brightly or differently coloured. The papillose callus below the column on the *Calanthe* lip, for example, is white in some specimens and bright orange in others. The red lip of *Eulophia orthoplectra* bears white crests and the white lip of *Nervilia humilis* bears a central yellow callus. In *Ansellia* and *Eulophia*, the raised ridges or lamellae extend lengthwise along the lip and above the veins, and in the latter genus they are variously crested or split into elongate papillae or hairs. In some species of *Liparis* and *Malaxis*, there are two smooth or hairy cushions on the base of the lip, and in a few species of *Eulophia* there are two erect and prominent calli in this position. In *Jumellea* and some species of *Angraecum*, there is a single, longitudinal, central keel, while in *Acampe* several papillose ridges on the lip are arranged transversely. In *Polystachya* and *Bulbophyllum*, many kinds of decorations occur: there are hairs, bumps, warts and crests, and sometimes a floury exfoliation, which sits loosely on the surface of the lip and offers a meal to a pollinating insect.

THE COLUMN

The smallest structure of the orchid flower, the column in its centre, provides the orchid taxonomist with many useful characters. From the orchid point of view it is simply the stalk that bears the pollination apparatus: it consists of the anther with its pollinia, the stigma or stigmatic cavity, and the rostellum. The latter is a sterile structure that both prevents self-pollination by its intermediate position between the anther and the stigma, and plays a part in cross-pollination by virtue of the sticky discs, or viscidia, that differentiate on its surface.

Two basic kinds of arrangement are seen in the African orchids. In the tribe Orchideae, the column bears the anther on one side, facing the incoming insect or the eye of the inquisitive botanist. The column is short and stout in most genera, and the bright yellow pollen is partly hidden, yet visible, within two slits or pouches on its surface. At its base there are sometimes one or two sterile staminodes, and a variously shaped rostellum. In *Brachycorythis, Habenaria, Bonatea, Disperis* and others, this is often three-lobed, extending laterally to form slender arms of varying length that each bears a sticky viscidium at its tip. In *Monadenia, Herschelia* and *Holothrix*, there is only a single viscidium, but in the other members of the tribe there are two. The number of stigmas present is similarly varied: two are found, sometimes as a sticky surface at the end of long projecting arms, in *Habenaria, Bonatea* and *Stenoglottis*. There are also two, more closely appressed to the column, in *Disperis, Corycium, Anochilus, Pterygodium* and *Evota*, while the rest of the genera in this tribe bear only a single, sticky, stigmatic surface.

Variations on this pattern are presented by the genus *Disa* and its allies, in some of which the upper part of the column is bent backwards so that the anther is held horizontally. In *Satyrium* the long, slender column has bent right over at its tip, so that the anther is held below the stigma and on the side of the column away from the over-arching lip. This arrangement ensures that the pollinia face the incoming insect, and it is the united sepals and petals, instead of the lip, which provide the landing-platform.

In the remainder of the orchids that occur in Africa, the column bears the anther near its tip, either on its upper surface, or on the vertical end of its blunt apex under an easily removable anther cap. In the length, shape and size of the column there is a wide range of variation: it is short and broad in *Polystachya*, and long and slender in *Barombia*, *Ancistrochilus* and *Liparis*; it is produced into a foot at its base in several genera, and armed with sharp points near its tip in *Bulbophyllum* and *Diceratostele*; in *Cheirostylis* and *Manniella*, it bears two terminal appendages, and keels are present on its front surface in *Hetaeria*. In most of these, and the other genera, the rostellum is fairly prominent, though again it is varied in shape and structure. In all the genera of the monopodial Aerangidinae, it sticks out across the surface of the stigma and may be simple or divided into two or three lobes. In several genera, its structure has been alluded to in their names, including *Ancistrorhynchus* (hooked rostellum), *Sphyrarhynchus* (hammer-shaped) and *Triceratorhynchus* (three-horned in both directions, like a trident). The stigma in these genera is usually a depression on the front of the column, glistening with receptive liquid, but is partly hidden by the protruding rostellum in *Angraecum, Mystacidium, Cyrtorchis* and others.

The detailed structure of the anther, in particular its attachment, structure, and the number and texture of its pollinia, has provided important criteria in subdividing the family Orchidaceae ever since its diversity was first fully appreciated by Lindley, the 'father of Orchidology', in the 1830s. In all the African orchids there is only a single anther, but two major divisions of the family depend on the way it is attached to the column.

In the Orchideae, the anther is broadly and firmly attached to the front of the column. The pollen is aggregated somewhat loosely into massulae, which in turn are agglutinated into two masses called pollinia. Elastic threads unite the massulae within each pollinium and an extension of these threads forms a stalk, the caudicle, by which the pollinium is attached to the sticky gland, or viscidium. The latter is a special contrivance, which is formed on the surface of the rostellum, whose function is to attach the entire pollinarium (pollinium, caudicle and viscidium) to the surface of any insect, bird, or other pollinating agent for transport to the stigma of another flower.

The rest of the African orchids have the anther attached to the apex of the column and a further major division concerns the character of the pollinia. In the tribes Neottieae, Cranichideae, Epipogeae, and Gastrodieae, the pollinia are made up of soft and mealy masses, one within each anther cell. In the other six tribes represented, the pollina are hard and waxy and vary in number from two to eight per flower. They are usually club-shaped, or laterally flattened. Often they are attached to each other by caudicles, and viscidia are usually present. In the Arethuseae there are four pollinia in *Phaius*, and eight in *Calanthe* and *Ancistrochilus*. The tribes Malaxideae and Dendrobieae are character-ised by naked pollinia, either two or four, and the genus *Stolzia*, which may belong in the latter tribe, is unusual in having eight, made up in pairs, four small and four large pollinia.

In the Vandeae, Polystachyeae and Cymbidieae, the rather hard pollinia, two or four, are always attached, by means of very short caudicles, to an upward extension of the viscidium known as the stipe. In many of the Aerangidinae this is divided into two, and sometimes two separate viscidia are also present. It is hardly necessary to investigate the anther of the Vandeae in order to be certain of the tribal affinity of its members, for they all exhibit a monopodial growth pattern that provides instantaneous recognition. But accurate observation and interpretation of these minute details at the apex of the column are essential to diagnose most of the thirty-eight genera that are currently recognised.

The genera of the Cymbidieae are easily recognised by their corms or pseudobulbs of several internodes, as well as by two thick pollinia that are attached to a wide viscidium. Again, the two genera so far recognised in the Polystachyeae have rather similar flowers, borne terminally above the apex of the pseudobulb, and at the apex of each column there are two pairs of pollinia under a tough, removable anther cap.

THE OVARY AND FRUIT

In all orchid flowers the ovary is inferior, situated below the sepals, petals, lip and column. Behind the open flower, the ovary and pedicel are sometimes hard to severalize but, at least in many resupinate flowers, the oblique arrangement of the ridges and grooves of the ovary is usually distinguishable. Sometimes the ovary is very hairy: it is glandular-hairy in *Cynorkis*, a generic characteristic, as also in *Platylepis*, and softly hairy in several species of *Holothrix*, *Habenaria*, *Ancistrochilus*, *Polystachya* and others.

The ovary in the flowers of African orchids bears its ovules on three fertile placentas arranged longitudinally along its inner walls. Although relatively undeveloped at flowering time, the fertile tissue grows and divides rapidly after receiving a hormonal stimulus when the pollen is deposited on the stigma. By the time the pollen grains have germinated, and their tubes have grown down through the tissues of the column and into the ovary, the ovules are fully mature and ready for fertilisation. This period is very variable; a few days and several months have both been recorded. Then there is often a second spurt of growth in the developing fruit as the fertilised ovules enlarge and ripen into seeds.

From the date of pollination to the release of ripe seeds is a time of very varied duration. In many terrestrial species there may be a delay only of weeks, while in most epiphytic species the period is several months. The time required for maturation of the seeds varies with the species, and sometimes with the individual, and clearly is at least partly dependent on growing conditions. In several species of *Aerangis* that have been studied closely in recent years, the period has varied from six weeks to nine months, but in the majority of species it was six to eight months. In these and many other species that have been observed in cultivation, the larger fruits usually take longer to mature than the smaller ones, but this is not invariably the case.

Botanically, the ripe fruit is a capsule and releases its seeds through one or more vertical slits that appear longitudinally along its walls. The most common method of dehiscence takes place when three or six slits are formed, and this has been observed in species of *Ansellia*, *Eulophia*, *Satyrium* and many other terrestrial genera. The slits appear between thickened valves or ribs of the capsule, which separate except at their tips. In all the members of the Vandeae that have been observed as yet, only one slit occurs, on the side of the capsule that is closest to the ground.

In all the capsules that have so far been examined, special expulsive hairs are present on the inner face of the valves. These hairs are hygroscopic and move sharply about when there are local changes in humidity. Eventually, they become detached from the capsule at their base and their movements, both earlier and subsequently, help to expel the seeds.

Most of the capsules observed in terrestrial species are held erect, though in the larger plants of *Eulophia, Acrolophia, Epipactis* and a few species of *Habenaria*, they are pendulous. In many epiphytic species the flowers are borne on pendent racemes or spikes and the fruits that develop on these are often held at right angles to the rachis, although they may sometimes be held erect or are pendulous. In a few genera, the pedicel elongates conspicuously during fruit formation, carrying the developing capsules some distance into the air away from the plant, perhaps to achieve more efficient seed dispersal thereby. Among terrestrial species, the saprophytic genera *Auxopus* and *Didymoplexis* exhibit this trait, the elongation of the pedicel being particularly exaggerated, to 15 or 20 cm, in the latter genus. Among the epiphytic species, a much smaller elongation has been observed in several species of *Bulbophyllum* and in *Oberonia*, both genera which bear relatively small flowers rather closely arranged in a dense spike. In the single-flowered species of *Nervilia*, it is the peduncle that elongates considerably in the fruiting stage.

The capsules vary considerably in size, shape and colour, but details about them are rarely recorded and little known. The largest among the African orchids are probably those of *Ansellia*, or of *Eulophia horsfallii*, both of which resemble a hen's egg in shape and size. Capsules in the genus *Aerangis* are usually long and narrow, sometimes up to fifteen times longer than the ovary from which they develop, but only three or four times greater in diameter. Many capsules are ellipsoid, some almost round, and others oblong or obovoid. Often they retain the remains of the flower at their apex. The column, which sometimes becomes greatly toughened and beak-like, is always present, but other parts of the perianth may also remain, making identification of the plant possible and definite even in the fruiting stage.

The capsules vary in colour as well as in shape, from species to species, and during the course of their maturation. Green ovaries develop into green fruits, as a rule, and brownish ones into brown capsules, but by the time the seeds are shed the outer tissues have died and dried to blackish-brown, or to a dull, straw-coloured yellow.

The epiphytic orchids produce far fewer fruits in proportion to the number of flowers than do the terrestrial species. This may be due to the small flowers of many terrestrials, or to their being more crowded on the rachis and visited by many more insects which are in greater abundance near the ground. Or it may be caused by hygroscopic changes within the flower making it possible for the erect pollinia to fall forward on to the stigma of terrestrial species and for self-pollination to occur. Some terrestrial species, and a very few epiphytes, are habitually self-pollinating, but most of the epiphytes are self-incompatible, so that even if self-pollination occurs and ovary-swelling begins, no seed is produced in the aborted fruit.

Figure 4   *African Orchid Flowers I*

1   Habenaria malacophylla: a, *plan of an inflorescence, a raceme, each flower supported by a spreading bract;* b, *single flower, face view (x3);* c, *part of a dissected flower to show the dorsal sepal, two-lobed petal, lateral sepal, and three-lobed lip with an inflated spur at its base (x5);* d, *column face view (left) and side view, sepals, petals and lip removed, the stigmatic surfaces visible at the tips of the short arms that project forward above the lip (x10);* e, *pollinarium with many massulae of pollen grains, long slender caudicle and small round viscidium (x20);* f, *fruit with twisted pedicel and the remains of the flower at its apex (x1). Dissections from a living plant collected in Natal,* Stewart 1788.

2   Holothrix scopularia: a, *plan of an inflorescence, a raceme with secund flowers;* b, *single flower, side view (x5);* c, *part of a dissected flower to show the many lobed lip with a short spur at its base, lateral sepal with hairy margin, three-lobed petal and intermediate sepal (x5);* d, *column, face view (left) and side view (x20);* e, *two pollinaria with many massulae of pollen grains, short caudicles and round viscidia (x20);* f, *fruit (x2). Dissections from a herbarium specimen at Natal University,* Stewart 2059.

3   Brachycorythis ovata: a, *plan of an inflorescence, a raceme with many flowers partially concealed among the bracts;* b, *single flower, face view (x2);* c, *part of a dissected flower to show the dorsal sepal, petal, lateral sepal and lip which is three-lobed at the base and the apex (x3);* d, *column, face view (left) and side view to show the attachment of the lip and details of its hypochile, sepals and petals removed (x7);* e, *pollinarium, with closely packed massulae of pollen grains, stout caudicle and small viscidium (x10);* f, *fruit (x1). Dissections from a herbarium specimen at Natal University,* Stewart 2148.

4   Schizochilus gerrardii: a, *plan of an inflorescence, a raceme with an inverted apex;* b, *single flower, face view (x5);* c, *dissected flower to show the dorsal sepal, paired petals, paired lateral sepals, which are larger, and three-lobed lip (x5);* d, *column, face view (left), and side view with lip to show the shape and position of the spur (x10);* e, *pollinarium, with many small massulae, long slender caudicle and small viscidium (x10);* f, *fruit, with the remains of the flower at its apex, dehiscing along three valves (x3). Dissections from herbarium specimens at Natal University,* Hilliard and Burtt 8418 and 9939.

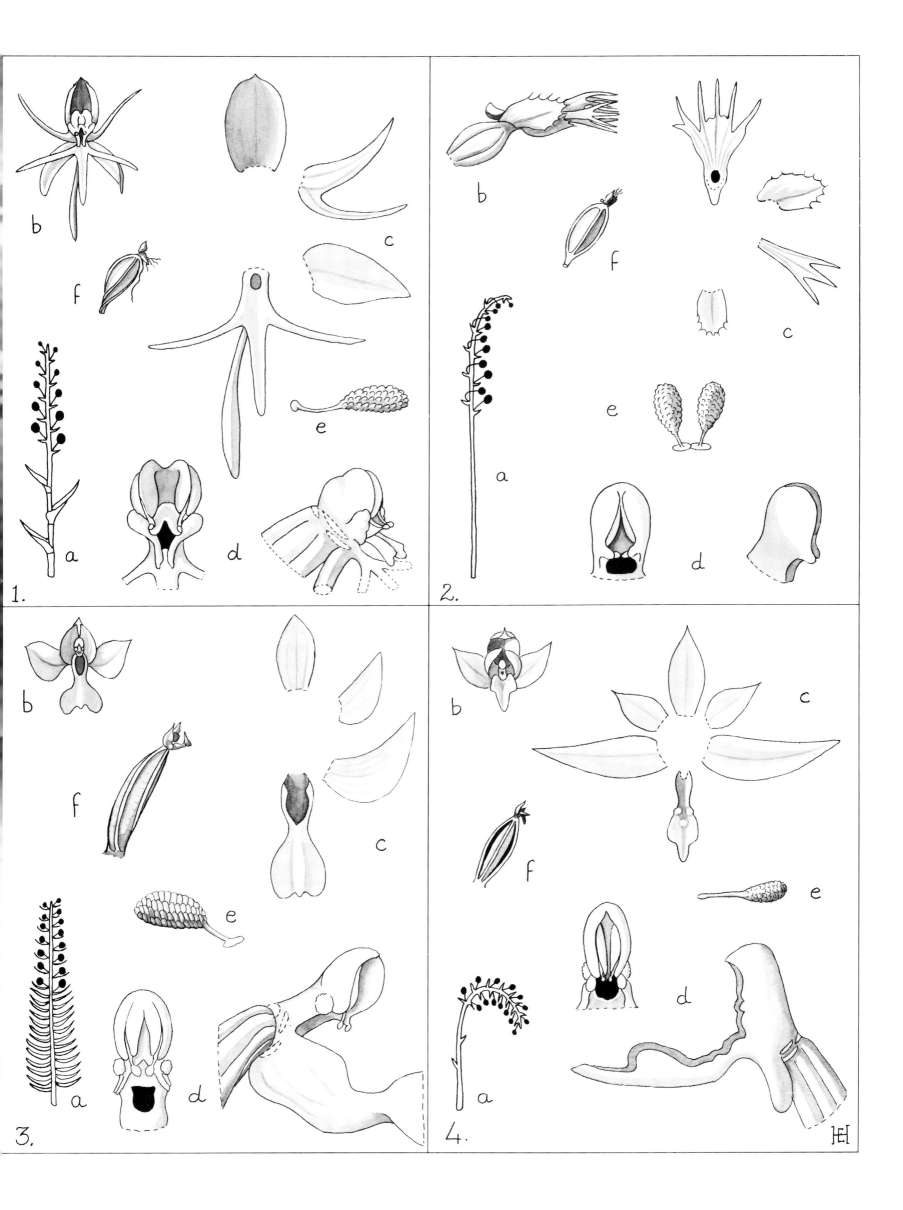

Figure 5   African Orchid Flowers II

1   Disa cooperi: a, *plan of an inflorescence, a terminal raceme;* b, *single flower, side view, showing the hood-shaped dorsal sepal with long spur (x1);* c, *part of a dissected flower to show the spurred dorsal sepal, petal, lateral sepal and lip (x1.5);* d, *column, side view, to show the anther held more or less horizontally behind the sloping stigmatic surface (x7);* e, *pollinarium, with large, densely packed massulae, slender caudicle and round viscidium (x7);* f, *fruit, with the remains of the flower at its apex (x1). Dissections from a herbarium specimen at Natal University,* Stewart 2151.

2   Satyrium longicauda: a, *plan of an inflorescence, a terminal raceme with deflexed bracts;* b, *single flower, face view, one spur partially removed (x3);* c, *part of a dissected flower to show the dorsal sepal with the spurs at its base cut off, petal, lateral sepal and narrow lip (x4);* d, *column, side view (left) and face view, with its tip inverted so that the anther is held below the broad, plate-shaped stigma (x5);* e, *pollinarium, with many massulae of pollen grains, long caudicle and large viscidium (x10);* f, *fruit, with the remains of the flower at its apex (x1). Dissections from a herbarium specimen at Natal University,* Stewart 1792.

3   Disperis johnstonii: a, *plan of an inflorescence, a few-flowered raceme;* b, *single flower, face view (x3);* c, *part of a dissected flower to show the narrow dorsal sepal, broad petal which is attached to the dorsal sepal along its upper margin, and paired lateral sepals (drawn from the back to show the spurs half way along their length) (x3.5);* d, *column and lip, the latter upturned and attached to the column for the length of its basal claw and with a two-lobed, papillose appendage at the point where it bends back on itself; the slender blade ends in a papillose limb projecting forwards in front of the column; one of the quiver-shaped sacs in which the pollinia are housed is visible at the side of the column with a slender, curved rostellum arm projecting forwards from it above the stigma (x9);* e, *pollinarium, large massulae of pollen grains attached to a broad caudicle bearing a small viscidium at its tip (x16);* f, *fruit, with the remains of the flower at its apex (x1). Dissections from preserved material at Natal University,* Stewart 2050.

4   Calanthe sylvatica: a, *plan of an inflorescence, a raceme with small bracts;* b, *single flower, face view (x1.5)* c, *part of a dissected flower to show the dorsal sepal, petal, lateral sepal, and four-lobed lip with a spur at its base, the basal claw of the lip which is fused with the column not shown (x1.5);* d, *column and base of lip, face view, to show the conspicuous callus on the lip in front of the opening to the spur (x5);* e, *pollinarium, consisting of eight elongated pollinia attached to a small disc-shaped viscidium (x10);* f, *fruit, with a long slender pedicel (x1). Dissections from a living plant collected in Natal,* Stewart 146–75, *presented to the author by* Olive Hilliard.

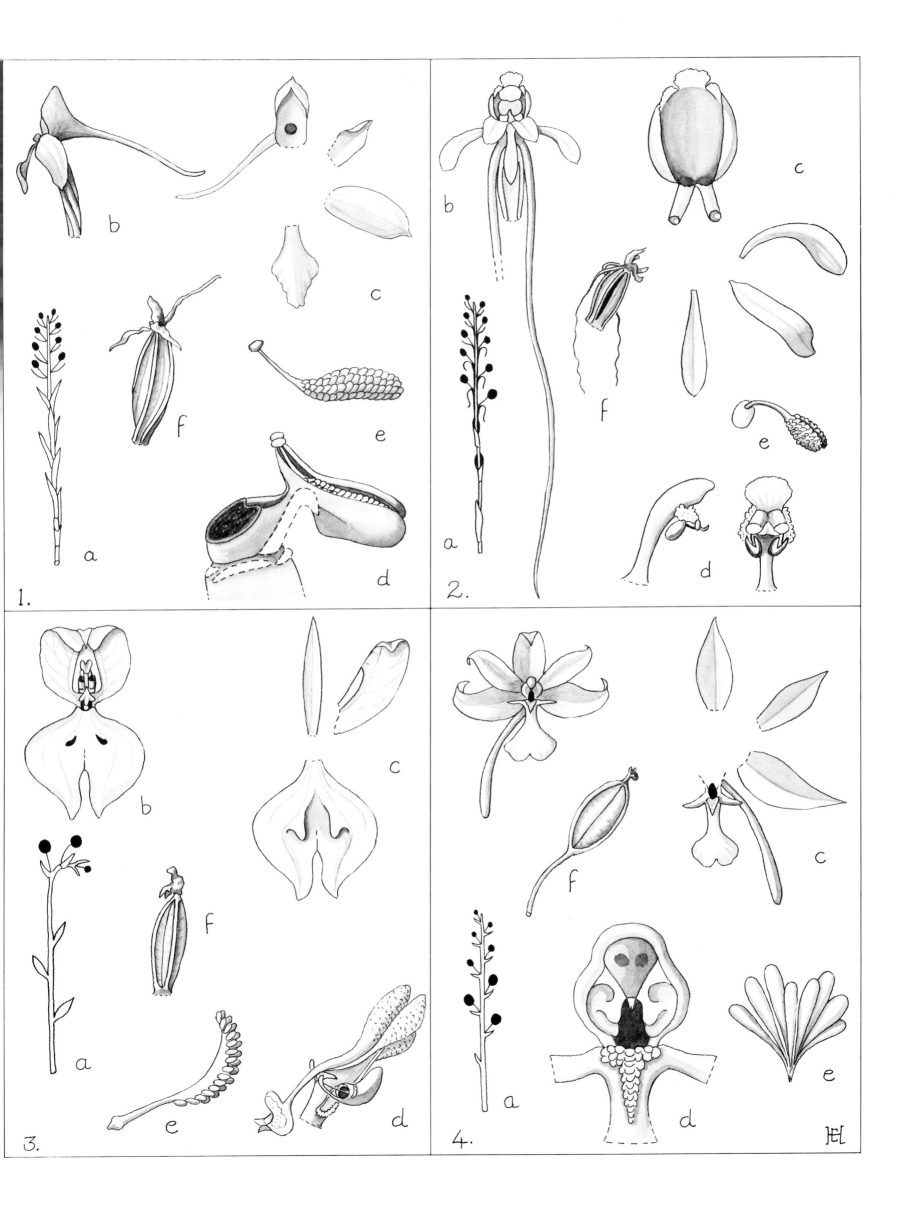

Figure 6   African Orchid Flowers III

1   Liparis bowkeri: a, *plan of an inflorescence, a raceme, each flower supported by an upright bract;* b, *single flower, face view (x3);* c, *part of a dissected flower to show the dorsal sepal, narrow petal, broad lateral sepal, and lip (x4);* d, *tip of column, the beaked anther cap at the top reveals two pairs of pollinia above the narrow rostellum which separates them from the stigmatic cavity; two conspicuous drops of moisture were present in the young flower dissected for this drawing (x20);* e, *one pair of pollinia, separated to show their triangular outline, concave inner surface (left) and convex outer surface (right) (x20);* f, *fruit, with a twisted pedicel, the remains of the flower at its apex (x1). Dissections from a living plant collected in Natal,* Stewart 1985.

2   Bulbophyllum scaberulum: a, *plan of an inflorescence, a raceme, the rachis expanded on two sides to form a flattened, knife-shaped structure, along which the pedicellate flowers are borne in the axils of bracts, usually along a line nearer to the upper margin than the lower;* b, *single flower, face view, with the hinged lip falling forward (x5);* c, *part of a dissected flower to show the dorsal sepal, narrow petal, broad and striped lateral sepal, and lip (x5);* d, *column, side view (right) sepals and petals removed to show the hinged lip at the base of its extended foot, and face view (x7);* e, *pollinia, two pairs of two unequal pollinia with no viscidium (x10);* f, *fruit (x1);* g, *anther cap with the pollinia in position on its inner surface (x10). Dissections from a living plant collected in Transkei,* Stewart 1608.

3   Acampe praemorsa: a, *plan of an inflorescence, a panicle with a thickened axis and few branches;* b, *single flower, face view (x3);* c, *part of a dissected flower to show the dorsal sepal, petal and lateral sepal, all thickened and somewhat concave, and the fleshy three-lobed lip (x3);* d, *column, face view, showing the very deeply recessed stigmatic surface, and pointed teeth on either side of the anther cap (x8);* e, *pollinarium, front view (right) and back view revealing two pairs of unequal pollinia (x10);* f, *fruit, which has dehisced along three ribs (x1);* g, *column and lip in side view, the sepals and petals removed, showing the shallow spur or sac at the base of the lip (x3). Dissections from a living plant collected in Zaïre,* Stewart 124–73, *presented to the author by Heather Campbell.*

4   Angraecum eichleranum: a, *sketch of a plant to show the origin of the one-flowered inflorescences, each arising below an adventitious root;* b, *single flower (x1);* c, *pedicel, ovary, and funnel-shaped lip, side view, sepals and petals removed (x1);* d, *column, side view (right), showing the triangular lobes of the rostellum below the anther cap, and viewed from below (left), showing the deep stigmatic cavity below the rostellum (x5);* e, *pollinarium, with two large pollinia borne on a single short stipe above a large heart-shaped viscidium (x10). Drawn from a living plant,* Stewart 19–77, *presented to the author by Douglas McMurtry.*

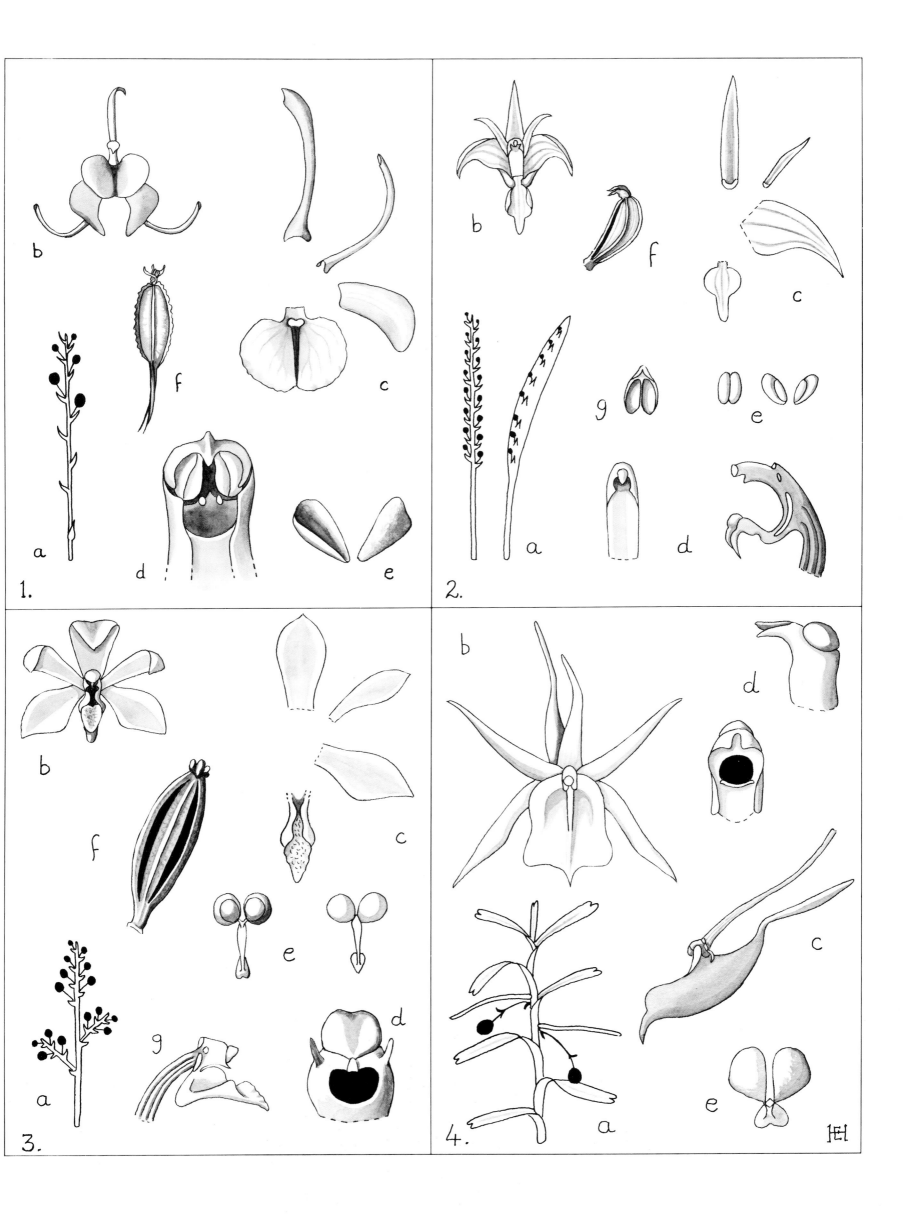

Figure 7   African Orchid Flowers IV

1   Aerangis mystacidii: a, *plan of an inflorescence, a pendent raceme with zigzag rachis;* b, *single flower, face view (x1.5);* c, *part of a dissected flower to show the dorsal sepal, petal and lateral sepal, all rather similar, and the lip with an elongated spur at its base (x2.5);* d, *column, face view, with the anther cap lifted to reveal the twin pollinia; the narrow and elongated rostellum lobe projects downwards in front of the large square stigmatic surface and bears an oval viscidium and long slender stipe on its upper surface (x7);* e, *pollinarium removed from the flower, the hygroscopic stipe becomes shorter by spirally twisting (x7);* f, *fruit, with the remains of the flower at its apex (x1). Dissections from a living plant collected in Zimbabwe,* Stewart 30–78, *presented to the author by Jane Browning.*

2   Ypsilopus longifolius *subspecies* erectus: a, *plan of an inflorescence, an arching raceme with small bracts;* b, *single flower, face view, lateral sepals and petals completely reflexed (x2);* c, *part of a dissected flower to show the dorsal sepal, petal, lateral sepal and lip with an elongated spur at its base (x3);* d, *column, face view, with the elongated rostellum lobe projecting downwards in front of the broad stigmatic surface (x10);* e, *pollinarium, with narrowly cordate viscidium, Y-shaped stipe and globose pollinia (x25);* f, *fruit, with the remains of the flower at its apex (x1). Dissections from material preserved at Natal University, collected in Zimbabwe,* Ashton 755.

3   Cyrtorchis arcuata: a, *plan of an inflorescence, a pendent raceme with large boat-shaped bracts;* b, *single flower, face view (x1);* c, *part of a dissected flower to show the dorsal sepal, petal, lateral sepal and lip with an S-shaped spur at its base (x1);* d, *column, with a large rhomboid anther cap (lifted on the right to reveal two pollinia each with its own stipe) and long, pointed rostellum lobe, pointing downwards into the mouth of the spur and almost occluding the stigmatic surface (x7);* e, *pollinarium, showing the broad viscidium that wraps over the edges of the rostellum lobe and one hygroscopic stipe supporting an ovoid pollinium (x10);* f, *fruit, with the remains of the flower at its apex, dehiscing by a single slit along the lower surface (x1);* g, *column, side view (x6). Dissections from a living plant collected in Natal,* Stewart 228–72.

4   Mystacidium millarii: a, *plan of an inflorescence, a pendent raceme;* b, *single flower, face view, the sepals and petals curved forward to form a cup-shaped flower (x3);* c, *part of a dissected flower to show the dorsal sepal, petal, narrow lateral sepal, and the lip with a spur at its base (x3);* d, *column, with apical anther cap (lifted on the right to reveal two small pollinia each with its own slender stipe) and broad three-lobed rostellum; each narrow stipe is hidden in a cleft between the lobes of the rostellum (x10);* e, *pollinarium with round pollinium and broadly cordate viscidium (x20);* f, *fruit, with a twisted pedicel, the remains of the flower at its apex and a single slit for the release of seeds (x2). Dissections from a living plant collected in Natal,* Stewart 110–76, *presented to the author by Ann Duckworth.*

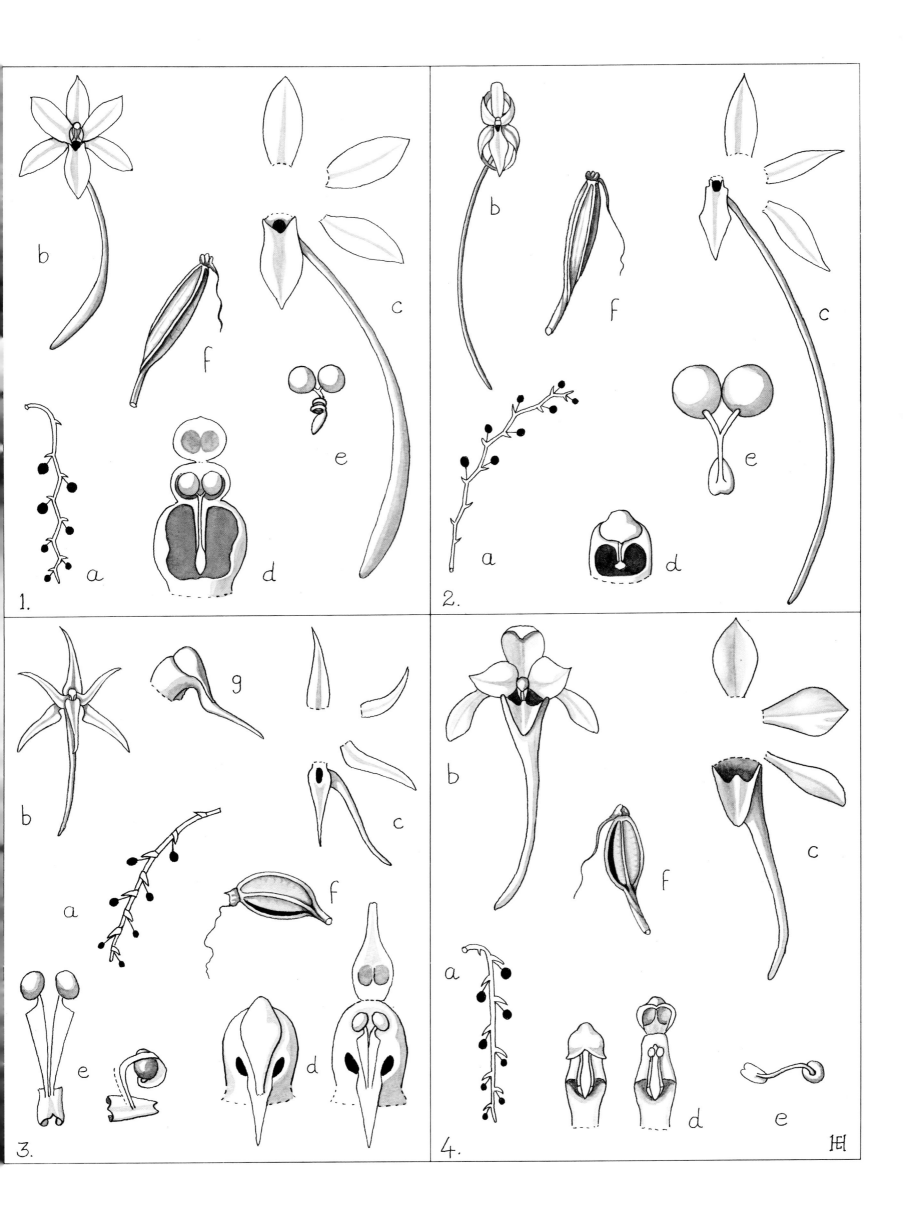

Figure 8   African Orchid Flowers V

1   Tridactyle bicaudata: a, *plan of an inflorescence arising in the axil of a leaf, an arching raceme;* b, *single flower, face view (x5);* c, *dissection of a single flower, with the dorsal sepal uppermost, paired petals and broader lateral sepals, and the three-lobed lip, with small auricles at its base on either side of the entrance to the elongated spur (x5);* d, *column, the anther cap lifted to reveal the pollinia (right); the triangular rostellum projects forward across the transversely elongated stigmatic surface, bearing the small round viscidium at its tip and the elongated stipe of the pollinarium on its upper surface (x10);* e, *pollinarium, consisting of a small round viscidium, single stipe, which becomes broader in the upper part, and two globose pollinia (x20);* f, *part of a fruiting axis bearing two capsules (x1). Dissections from a living plant collected in Transkei,* Stewart 1605.

2   Polystachya concreta: a, *plan of an inflorescence, a raceme or panicle with few branches near the base;* b, *single flower, front view (x5);* c, *part of a dissected flower to show the three-lobed lip, broad lateral sepal, narrow petal, and the intermediate sepal on the lower side of the flower (x5);* d, *column, face view, and with anther cap tilted forward (right) to reveal two pairs of pollinia, each pair borne on a short broad stipe but attached to a single viscidium (x10);* e, *pollinarium, consisting of four pollinia attached to a single narrow viscidium (x10);* f, *young fruit with remains of the flower at its apex (x1). Dissections from a living plant collected in Mozambique,* Stewart 161–75, *presented to the author by Kevin Rogers.*

3   Acrolophia cochlearis: a, *plan of an inflorescence, a panicle;* b, *single flower, face view, shown in the resupinate position but many flowers in the panicle have the lip uppermost (x3);* c, *part of a dissected flower to show the dorsal sepal, small petal, lateral sepal, and the broad lip with an undulate margin and a short spur at its base (x5);* d, *column, with the anther cap lifted to display the elongated rostellum, which the viscidium fits over, extending downwards across the stigmatic surface (x5);* e, *anther, consisting of the pollinarium (above) with two pollinia, broad stipe and viscidium, and the anther cap (below) which encloses the pollinia at the apex of the column (x10);* f, *fruit, showing part of the twisted pedicel (x1). Dissections from a herbarium specimen at Natal University,* Hilliard and Burtt 10847.

4   Eulophia horsfallii: a, *plan of an inflorescence, usually a long raceme;* b, *single flower, face view (x1);* c, *part of a dissected flower to show the narrow dorsal sepal, broad petal, narrow lateral sepal and the three-lobed lip with raised lamellae on the disc (x1);* d, *detached pollinarium and anther cap, the latter with twin horns at its apex, rear view (above), and column apex, front view (below), to show the position of the horned anther cap above the narrow rostellum and transverse stigmatic surface (x5);* e, *pollinarium with two pollinia attached to a broad stipe and viscidium (x5);* f, *fruit, dehiscing along three ribs (x1);* g, *side view of flower, sepals and petals removed, to show the twisted ovary and broad spur or mentum at the base of the lip and foot of the column (x1). Drawn from a herbarium specimen at Natal University,* Pooley 1715.

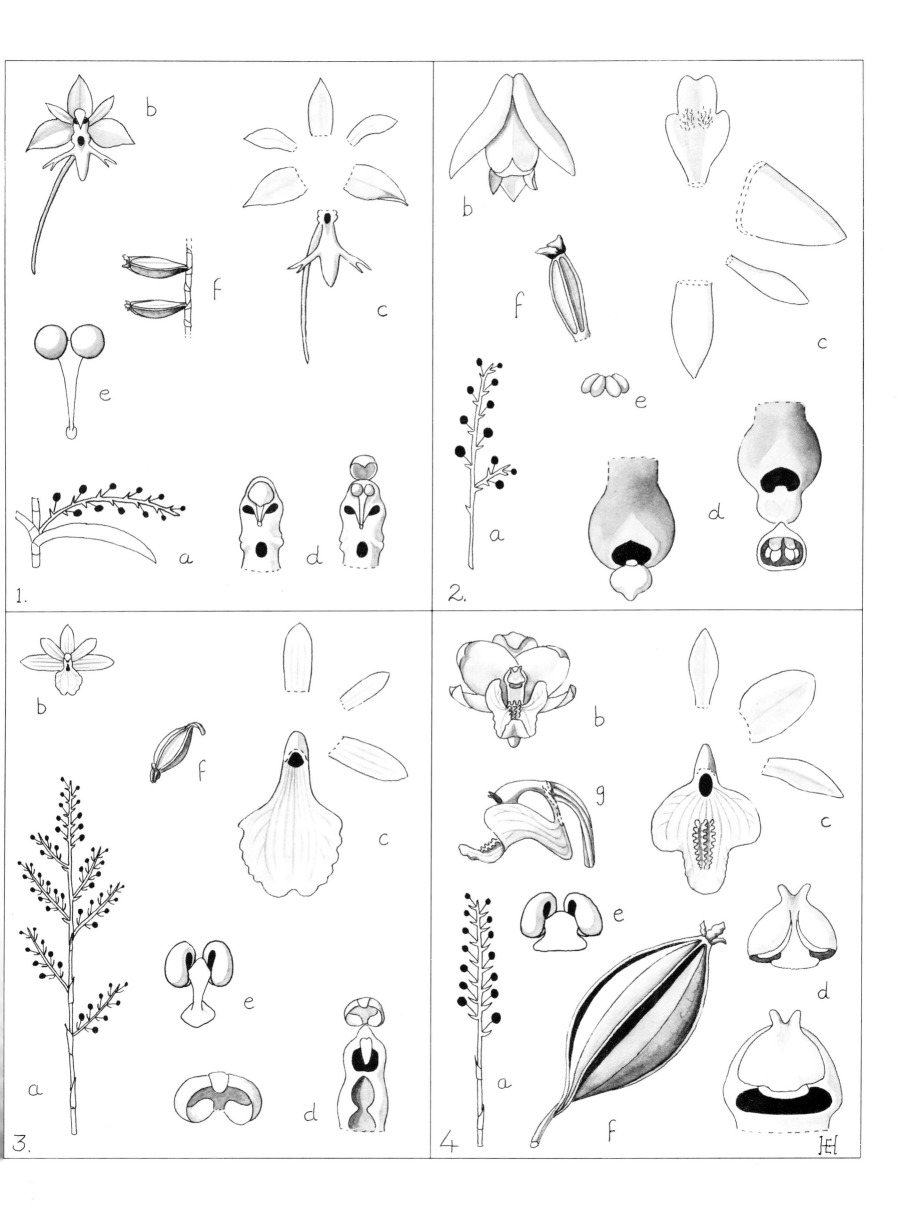

1.

2.

3.

4.

CHAPTER FOUR
Pollination

The symmetry and detail of orchid flowers indicate that they are designed to be pollinated by insects. The transfer from one flower to another of enormous numbers of pollen grains is essential for the fertilisation of the large number of ovules that are produced. To make transfer a more certain event, the minute pollen grains are united into masses, called pollinia, many of which have an adhesive disc, the viscidium, which unites them to their insect carrier for the requisite period of flight. The mechanisms that bring about this adhesion are many and varied, and the head, limbs, or body of the insect may be involved. At the same time, the complexity of the mechanism can enormously restrict the choice of pollen-carrier. The flowers are thus very specialised, or adapted, to particular visitors, and it is often the case that only one insect is able to pollinate any one particular species.

So the orchid flower is a gambler. If it is successful in attracting the desired insect, and that insect enters or emerges from the flower at the correct angle, one or more pollinia will be removed. But this packet of many pollen grains must be deposited with great precision on the rather circumscribed stigmatic surface of another flower. Pollen-reception is therefore also something of a gamble; often it requires movement of the pollinium on the insect during flight and, if it is sufficiently precise, this enables pollen deposition to occur when the next flower is visited. Because of the flower-constancy of many insects, both deposition and removal may be accomplished during one visit to a single flower. A careful estimate made by Charles Darwin indicated that the number of pollen grains in the single anther of *Orchis mascula* was 122,400 — six times more than required for the fertilisation of its ovules should successful pollination occur. Perhaps the all-or-nothing strategy of the orchid flower is not such a risky undertaking as it at first appears.

The flowers of African orchids offer many attractive devices to lure the pollinator into the correct position to achieve pollen removal or deposition. Scent, shape, and colour, combined with size, arrangement and position on the plant have been described already. These all play their part. But it is usually the promise of food, drink, or sex, or an advertisement indicating their probable availability, which plays the major role as an attractant.

As a group, orchid flowers use nectar as the chief allurement. It is produced in specialised tissues of the lip in many flowers, but in the spur of the dorsal sepal in the genus *Disa* and its allies, and in the lateral sepals of *Disperis*. The mentum at the foot of the column acts as a spur, or nectary, in *Polystachya*, and in *Bulbophyllum* and *Cirrhopetalum* nectar is produced in grooves on the surface of the lip. But probably not more than two-thirds of all orchid species produce nectar.

In many of the more primitive flowers, such as roses, the pollen is one of the chief attractants, offering a meal to the visiting insect for itself or its larvae. Pollen is produced in very limited quantities in orchids and in such a way that it is not readily available as food, but nectarless orchids are not above offering deceptive counterfeits, such as pseudopollen. A powdery mass, resembling the pollen of other flowers, is produced on the lip of several species of *Polystachya*. In *P. cultriformis* and *P. concreta* it is visible as large grains, perhaps arising from papillae that have become detached from the surface. Sometimes multicellular hairs break up into fragments filled with starch, or remain intact offering 'food hairs' that can be grazed. It has been assumed that hairs and scales on the surface of the lip of *Vanilla* species are also 'grazed' by bees, since they contain abundant reserves in the form of oil and sugars. The rather tough lamellae, or ridges, on the lip of *Eulophia horsfallii* apparently also supply food to bees who tear at them and avidly lick the ruptured surface.

For many insects, odours are the chief attractant, but very little is known of the nature of their effect. Some orchid flowers in Europe and South America attract only male bees and are important, ecologically, in assisting the insect to establish a territory. A few orchid flowers incite pseudocopulation, where the insect attempts to mate with the flower. Here shape, hairiness and colour of the flower combine with an odour produced by compounds similar to pheromones to effect the complete deception. These strategies have not yet been reported in the flowers of African orchids, but there are very few accurate records of observations of pollinating activities, so there may well be surprises in store when more studies have been made.

Orchids pollinated by bees are open during the day, and present their flowers horizontally, with a prominent lip for the insect to land on. They produce a sweet, fresh smell and are usually brightly coloured. Blue, violet, purple, yellow and white flowers are all attractive to bees. Often the flowers have obscure markings, in the form of nectar guides, that are beyond our range of vision but obvious to a bee who is sensitive to the ultraviolet range. Bees cannot perceive red, which may explain the relative rarity of this colour in flowers. They visit orchid flowers to obtain nectar but it is often hidden from them in specialised containers. Most observations of orchids pollinated by bees and other hymenoptera have been made in South America. In South Africa *Disa racemosa* and *Disa draconis* are both bee-pollinated, but there are surely many other orchids that are suitably coloured and scented to attract bees as well as these.

Flowers that are adapted for pollination by butterflies are also open during the day, provide a horizontal landing-place, and are vividly coloured, often in shades of red. They have a fresh, agreeable odour and produce nectar in long narrow tubes. Several species of *Disa*, in South Africa, are regularly pollinated by butterflies. The long narrow spur is situated near the top of the flower, on the dorsal sepal, and the rather broad lateral sepals act as a landing-platform. As soon as they are removed from the flower, the rather large pollinia, on elongated caudicles, fall forward under their own weight so that the pollen massulae are in the ideal position, below the head or thorax of the insect, for deposition on the stigma of the next flower the butterfly probes for a drink. *Disa uniflora* has been observed many times with its butterfly pollinator, *Meneris tulbaghia*, in action, and the similarly coloured, but smaller flowered, *Disa polygonoides* is also butterfly-pollinated.

The specialised features developed by flowers pollinated by moths include their size, or finely dissected shape, green or white coloration and crepuscular or nocturnal odour production. This odour is heavy and sweet, and may be produced in osmophores on the entire surface of the flower, or limited to certain parts, such as the petals in *Habenaria epipactidea*. Orchids pollinated by the hovering sphingid moths present no landing-place, but indicate their centre by their starry shape, whereas the ordinary moths, the noctuids and related families, require a turned-up landing-place from which to feed. Nectar is produced in abundance by all these flowers, particularly in the long spurs of species of *Habenaria* and its allies, and those of *Aerangis* and related genera. Often its level is apparent through the pellucid substance of the spur and sometimes it overflows on to the surface of the lip. The groove or keel on the lip may act as a tongue-guide, permitting penetration of the spur only to those insects who place their heads in the most appropriate position for pollen removal or deposition.

Several groups of birds act as pollinators of orchids in the western hemisphere. In Africa there are numerous species of sunbirds with long curved beaks: they are somewhat similar to the American humming-birds but are larger and heavier. As yet,

41

none of these birds has been reported as a pollinator of orchids in Africa, although sunbirds frequently pollinate species of *Dendrobium* in New Guinea, Java and in Singapore. It has been suggested that several species of *Disa* — *D. zeyheri*, *D. ferruginea* and *D. porrecta* — in South Africa exhibit most of the features that bird-pollinated flowers have evolved. They are vividly coloured in shades of red, but have no scent: birds, having almost no sense of smell, depend on sight to locate their food. The flowers are tubular, fairly hard in texture to resist the pressure of a probing beak, and the tube often extends into a spur that is abundantly supplied with nectar. Many bird-pollinated orchids bear a heavy callus or a strong fold of tissue on the lip, which forces the bird to push its beak against the column in order to gain access to the nectar. The similarity of the west African orchid, *Dicerotostele gabonensis*, to several South American species in *Elleanthus*, which are regularly pollinated by humming-birds, suggests that this species, too, may be pollinated by a bird.

Flies are regular pollinators of orchid flowers in many parts of Africa. The flowers concerned have mostly adopted a deception syndrome; they produce a smell that is similar to the creature's normal food, or breeding substrate, but rarely reward the insect with anything tangible. The odour of overripe fruit or rotting animal carcases is correlated with dull greenish or brownish-purple colours, sometimes with a brown, hairy or furry covering, with motile hairs that vibrate in the slightest whisper of wind, and with an intricate trapping mechanism to ensure that the insect's head or abdomen contacts the column in precisely the desired direction. *Bulbophyllum*, and its allied genera *Chaseëlla*, *Cirrhopetalum*, and perhaps *Stolzia*, all exhibit a delicately balanced lip which tips over like a seesaw on its fulcrum when the weight of the insect disturbs its equilibrium. The broad lateral sepals of *Cirrhopetalum*, and the wing-like rachis of all the species in the section *Megaclinium* of *Bulbophyllum*, provide a landing-place from which the fly can make a cautious and careful approach to the attractive features of the flower. It is even helped on its useful way by the sensitive hinge at the base of the lip. There are also fly-pollinated orchids in other genera, notably *Satyrium* and *Disa*. *Satyrium pumilum*, in the Cape, is particularly intriguing, in that the radial arrangement of the flowers, on a short stem near the ground, deceives the observer at first by its resemblance to many similarly coloured species of *Stapelia*, the carrion-scented flowers of the dicotyledonous family Asclepiadaceae, which are also pollinated by flies.

Sometimes beetles are attracted to the flowers which show the characteristics that are specialised for fly pollination. Beetles, and several plant bugs, have been observed on *Corycium nigrescens* with pollinia adhering to their legs and lower abdomen, but it is not certain that these have been successful pollinators. They may have been merely robbers.

Rather few orchids have been reported as regularly self-pollinating. In cultivation *Polystachya fusiformis* and *Stenoglottis fimbriata* regularly set seed without being pollinated and in the former species the flowers often do not open. But these activities have not been reported in other species as yet. In the wild there is usually such an abundance of insect life that it is often difficult to find flowers with their pollinia still intact when these are needed for study or illustration.

The mechanisms for the transfer of pollen to the stigma are thus many and varied, and in several plants more than one agency is equally acceptable. The arrival of pollen on the stigma is the stimulus for a rapid and striking series of events to begin. Within hours the flower begins to wilt, change colour, or shrink. Sometimes the column turns red and the sepals and petals swell. They may become fleshy and turn green, dull red, or a mixture of both. In *Angraecum eburneum* the sides of the lip fold over the column, sealing the flower against further insect visits, and in many species of *Aerangis* the side lobes of the column grow forward and bend towards the rostellum, holding the heavy pollinia in place on the stigmatic surface and protecting them from any possibility of displacement.

The physiological changes that have been demonstrated recently are less easy to observe but very important. In many orchids, pollination stimulates the production of a plant hormone that induces the completion of the ovule development in the inferior ovary. Thus energy is conserved, as ovules are fully prepared only when the promise of forthcoming fertilisation has been received. Pollen grains on the stigmatic surface germinate by sending narrow tubes down through the column towards the cavity of the ovary, causing a swelling and stiffening of the column that is always a concomitant feature of successful pollination.

CHAPTER FIVE

The Seed and Seedling

Orchids are notorious for the prodigality of their tiny seeds. Over a hundred years ago Darwin recorded an average of more than six thousand seeds in the capsule of a small British orchid, and reported another botanist's count of nearly two million in a *Maxillaria* from South America. The record seems to be held by another South American species, of the genus *Cycnoches*, which was reported by Rolfe, in 1909, to contain 3,770,000 seeds in a single capsule. Reliable counts of seed number in African orchid capsules are not available, but casual observations, in the field and laboratory, have indicated that plants in this continent are just as prolific as elsewhere.

The seeds observed so far are variable in size and shape, but mostly somewhat elongated, regularly extended on either side of the somewhat cylindrical centre. Aerodynamically, they present a beautiful shape, which, coupled with their extreme lightness, makes them ideal for dispersal by wind, sometimes over considerable distances.

The largest seed encountered as yet is that of *Disa uniflora*, which is almost spherical, has a very large embryo and a shrunken seed-coat, and may be as much as one millimetre in diameter. Possibly the stream-side habitat of this species has in some way been responsible for the enlarged seed and short seedling life of this delightful species. The seeds of many species are only one tenth of this size and most are somewhat intermediate.

Fertile seeds are usually yellow or brown, and sterile seeds, lacking embryos or containing only aborted ones, are white. Viability can be confirmed by viewing through a microscope: the globular or ellipsoid embryo is easily discernible within the inflated net of the single layer of cells of the seed-coat.

Germination of the seed takes place rapidly as the embryo absorbs moisture, swells and bursts through the seed-coat. In some species, the invasion of the seed-coat and embryo by the threads of a fungal mycelium takes place even before this stage. In others, the fungus seeks entry to the protocorm, the first-formed stage of the new plant, through one of the slender hairs that cover its surface. It seems likely that the primary intentions of the fungus are entirely selfish — the digestion of the orchid embryo for its own energy requirements being its aim. But the orchid embryo is canny: it permits the presence of the fungal hyphae within its territory, but limits the extension of the would-be parasite by producing 'warding-off compounds', highly selective fungicides called phytoalexins. Thus it controls the volume of growth of the fungus in a manner somewhat similar to the way in which antibodies of animals halt the multiplication of organisms causing infectious disease. But then it capitalises on its incursor, and obtains the sugars, vitamins and minerals for its own growth from it. A fluid supply is always available from the mainly saprophytic fungus, whose extensive mycelium obtains these materials by enzymatic digestion of the many items of plant and animal litter in the surface layers of the soil.

Clearly, in the wild, the chances of a seed coming into contact with the mycelium of a fungus it can control are slight and this, perhaps, is the reason for the enormous production of seeds. But should invasion by a suitable hypha be achieved, and establishment of the symbiotic relationship between the fungus and the orchid be successful, then the orchid embryo is able to develop into a protocorm and, subsequently, a seedling.

Many terrestrial species have colourless protocorms when germinated in the laboratory, as they probably also do in the field where the seeds germinate in the soil in the absence of light. Others behave as the epiphytic protocorms do, by becoming green immediately. Following protocorm development, the next stage produced by the terrestrial species is a short, thickened structure, a tuber, rhizome or pseudobulb. The advantages of this method of development are obvious: the young plant now has sufficient reserves to remain dormant during the unfavourable conditions that alternate with the growing season, and will produce the familiar tiny shoot, with its adventitious roots, at the beginning of the next rainy period.

When the protocorm or seedling has become green, photosynthetic, and large enough to develop its own absorptive roots, it can either continue its life alone, restricting the presence of its symbiotic fungus to a distinct layer in the cortex of the root, or prevent the internal penetration of hyphae entirely, retaining them only in an external layer surrounding the roots or tubers. Thus the developing orchid plantlet can still make nutritional use of the association, but it is doubtful whether the fungus derives much benefit from it.

Recent observations indicate that symbiosis, or it may be more correctly termed parasitism on the part of the orchid, is not essential for germination in all species. The relatively large seeds of *Disa uniflora*, and of several species of *Liparis*, are pale green when they leave the capsule, and on a suitable substratum they become green and protocormous almost immediately. Provided the environmental conditions, particularly moisture availability, remain favourable, their development into seedlings proceeds well without a partner, and the *Disa*, at least, can be grown to flowering size in little more than two years. Volunteer seedlings of *Cynorkis* and *Bonatea* have appeared and grown to flowering size, not only in the pots occupied by the parent plants, but also in other parts of the author's greenhouse where fungicides are used routinely.

The time taken by other African orchid seedlings to reach flowering size has rarely been recorded, either in nature or in the laboratory. There are records of laboratory-grown species flowering while still in the flask, particularly of some of the smaller epiphytes such as *Aerangis*, in only eighteen months from sowing. Growers and hybridisers of terrestrial species in South Africa regularly obtain flowers in the greenhouse within three years. Many seedlings achieve this celerity under optimum conditions, but others grow very slowly, and often many years elapse between the hopeful gathering and dispersal of seeds and the first appearance of long-awaited flowers.

PART II
Selected Species of African Orchids

PLATE I
Platylepis glandulosa

A creeping terrestrial plant with robust stems and delicate leaves. The stems lie at ground level, or in the upper layers of soft forest soil, usually in situations at the edge of seepage zones where the substratum is perennially wet. They bear few roots with numerous fine, woolly hairs. Each stem tip curves upwards and is crowned with a rosette of broad, petiolate leaves. Their life is short-lived and by the time the spicate inflorescence appears from the heart of the leafy crown, the lower leaves are already beginning to age, change colour and fall. The flowering stem is clothed with sterile bracts for most of its length and these, together with the floral bracts, the ovary and the outer surface of the sepals, are all densely covered with white glandular hairs. Between this cottony covering the white flowers emerge; sometimes they are tinged with pink or brown, more often they look rather greenish. The dorsal sepal is somewhat hooded and partially conceals the rounded petals. The lateral sepals are briefly united at the base and spread sideways on either side of the simple lip. The latter is united with the column in its basal half and has two shallow sacs or gibbosities at its base. The anther is situated on the upper side of the column, behind its tip, and covered by a pointed, removable cap. It encloses four mealy pollinia that are attached to a simple elongated viscidium. *Plant life size; flower x10; lip x10; pollinia x12*

Platylepis glandulosa (Lindley) Reichenbach *filius* in *Linnaea*, **41**: 62 (1877)
Notiophrys glandulosa Lindley in *Journal of the Linnean Society*, **6**: 138 (1862)

When it is not in flower this orchid can be mistaken quite easily for a member of the family Commelinaceae. Its broad, ovate leaves with narrow, sheathing petioles are remarkably similar to those of several species of *Commelina* and *Aneilema* with which it sometimes grows. The terminal inflorescence, resembling a green, furry cone at the top of a stiff upright stalk, is very distinctive. Its tiny flowers are somewhat insignificant, but detailed study will reveal to the careful observer that this orchid is more like several European and American genera, such as *Spiranthes* and *Goodyera*, than others from the African continent. When the English orchidologist, John Lindley, first described this species in 1862, he was aware of this similarity and classified this plant in his genus *Notiophrys*, a name that refers to the southern origin of this orchid (from the Greek, *notios*: south, and *Ophrys*: a well-known European orchid genus). Comparative study by the German botanist, Professor H.G. Reichenbach, revealed, however, that this species actually belongs in the genus *Platylepis*, which had been proposed by the French botanist Achille Richard in 1828, long before *Notiophrys* was described.

This species is now known to be very widespread in Africa. It has been collected in many forested areas, between Portuguese Guinea in the west and Sudan in the east, and it extends southwards as far as the warm coastal forests of Natal in South Africa. The specimen illustrated here was collected near Lake St Lucia by Elsa Pooley, and has provided something of a challenge in cultivation. The plants are fairly easy to maintain in well-drained compost, in warm and humid but deeply shaded conditions, usually under the greenhouse bench. But flowering is somewhat erratic, and exactly what stimulus is required to trigger the development of the inflorescence from the stem apex is not known. Recent observations, at St Lucia and elsewhere in Natal, have indicated that the flowering period is equally variable in the wild. Flowers have appeared in September, January and March, in the same plant population in different years. The onset of flowering may be related to the start of the summer rains, which are notoriously unreliable in many parts of Africa, but this would hardly be the cause in cultivated plants, which show a similar flowering pattern although they are regularly supplied with overhead water.

E. F. Hennessy

PLATE 2
Stenoglottis fimbriata

A terrestrial plant with a basal rosette of leaves appearing annually above a perennial cluster of root tubers. The closely spaced leaves are lanceolate and elongated, tapering at both ends, with a crisped or undulate margin, and a number of purplish spots, sometimes very large ones, on both surfaces. The erect flowering stem is leafless, but in its lower part it bears a few scattered sheaths that are also spotted. The flowers vary in size and are often rather small; they are arranged in a loose, one-sided raceme, which continues to elongate as the flowers open over a period of several months. The dorsal sepal is slightly narrower than the lateral ones and all are lilac pink or paler in colour, sometimes with darker spots towards the tips. The petals are shorter than the sepals and are held erect so that they enclose the column. The three-lobed lip is a conspicuous feature of the flower. It is usually paler than the sepals but more densely·spotted. The lateral lobes are usually shorter than the central lobe and diverge from it; often they are slightly toothed, or almost subdivided. The column bears two large pollinia, each enclosed in a pouch-like slit on its face. The club-shaped stigma lobes protrude from the column, below the anther, and there is also a pair of glandular staminodes at its base.

Plants life size; flower, side view x3, face view x4; column x16; single pollinium x22

Stenoglottis fimbriata Lindley in Hooker, *Companion to the Botanical Magazine*, **2**: 210 (1837)

The small genus *Stenoglottis* was proposed by the English orchidologist, John Lindley, and based on the species illustrated here. The specimen he saw was collected by the German explorer and traveller, J.F. Drège, between the Umzimvubu and Umsikaba rivers in the part of Southern Africa that is now included in Transkei.

Our specimen came from rocks in the forest clothing the steep valley sides of the river Umzimvubu, not far from its mouth at Port St Johns. It seems very likely, therefore, that it is similar to the one seen by Lindley, although the petals and side lobes of the lip are not laciniate as he described them.

This pretty orchid was illustrated in colour as long ago as 1870 when Sir Joseph Hooker described it in *Curtis's Botanical Magazine*. He called it the 'Spotted Natal Orchid' in allusion to the purplish spots which are often present on the leaves. The specimen Hooker saw was grown in England, at Reigate in Surrey, in the rich and varied plant collection of W. Wilson Saunders, which included many orchids.

More than twenty years later Hooker described *Stenoglottis longifolia* in the same publication. His diagnosis was accompanied by another very fine plate, prepared from plants sent to Kew by J. Medley Wood, the first Curator of the Durban Botanic Gardens in Natal. Wood's plants were collected in the Ngoye Forest, and they are easily distinguished from *S. fimbriata* by their larger size, longer leaves, longer inflorescences with many more, larger flowers (always more than one hundred) and by the lip apex, which is usually five-lobed.

Both species can be found in Natal today, but while the fine and vigorous *S. longifolia* seems to be very limited in its distribution, *S. fimbriata* is now known to be very widespread and extremely variable. Luxuriant plants from the coastal forests approach *S. longifolia* in size, but the flower structure is always rather different; miniature plants bearing only a few flowers can be found on rocks near mountain streams; and there are many intermediates. In many specimens the flowers are self-pollinated, but this never happens in *S. longifolia*. The widespread *S. fimbriata* extends its range beyond Natal, south into the Cape Province of South Africa, and northwards as far as the southern highlands of Tanzania. In the wild it is found in very shallow soil or compost on rocks and as an epiphyte on mossy tree trunks. It responds very well to cultivation in a shallow pot with very good drainage, but requires a short dry season when the leaves die down until the new season's growth begins.

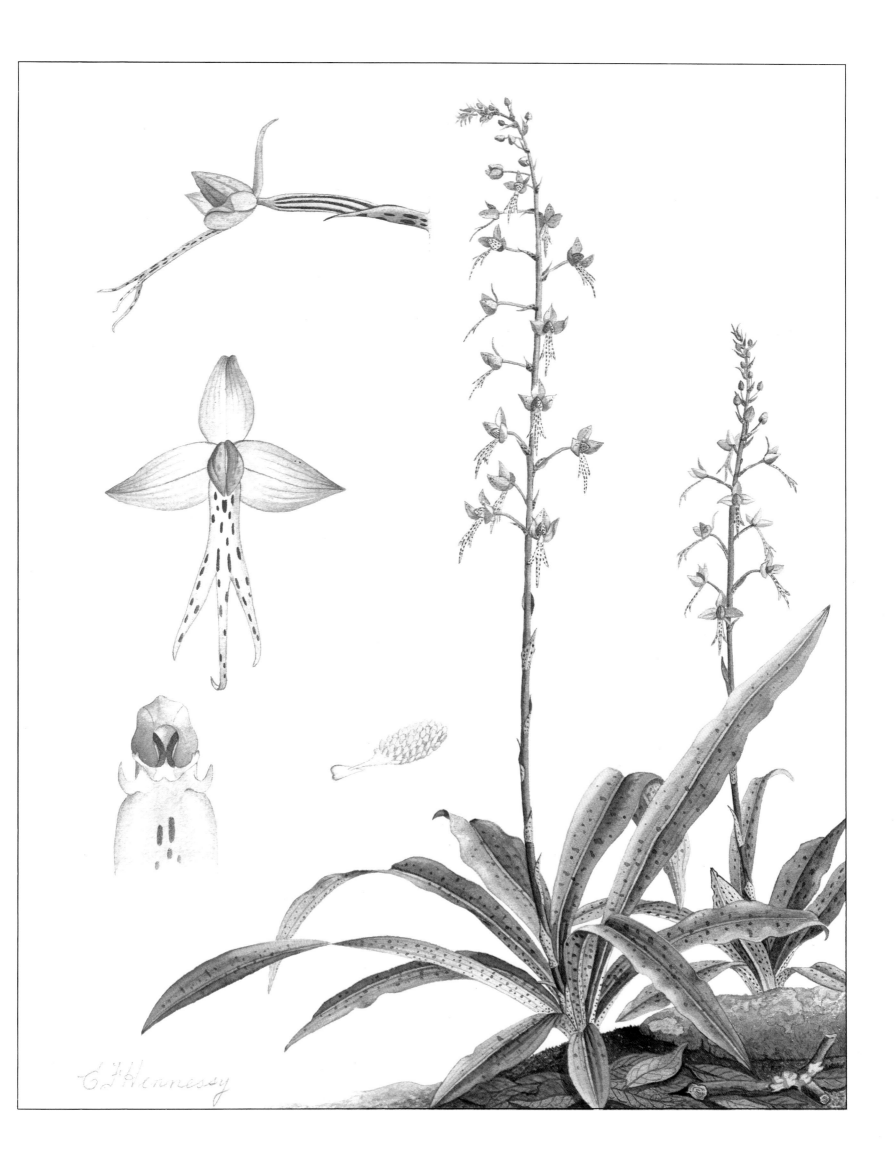

C.J.Hennessy

PLATE 3
Habenaria clavata

A robust terrestrial herb that is entirely glabrous except for the roots. The erect leafy stem arises annually above a single fleshy tuber, sometimes accompanied by a sterile leafy shoot. The broad leaves clasp the stem and only the upper ones spread away from it to any extent. The inflorescence is rather lax, bearing five to sixteen green flowers on long, nearly erect pedicels. As the rather bulbous bud opens, the dorsal sepal remains erect and the broader lateral sepals reflex away from the rest of the flower and roll up so that they are hard to distinguish from the ovary. The petals are characteristic and curiously two-lobed. The upper lobe is narrow and more or less attached to the outer margin of the dorsal sepal on each side, while the lower lobe is much stouter and longer and curves outwards and upwards, so that together the lower lobes resemble a pair of horns projecting from the centre of the flower. The three-lobed lip is extended at its base into a club-shaped spur, which often has its swollen tip tucked into the leafy bract that supports the flower. The short column bears two bright yellow anther cells on its face and the long white stigmas project forward in front of it above the surface of the lip, immediately below the slender side lobes of the rostellum.   *Plants life size*

Habenaria clavata (Lindley) Reichenbach *filius* in *Flora*, **48**: 180 (1865)
Bonatea clavata Lindley in Hooker, *Companion to the Botanical Magazine*, **2**: 208 (1837)

This species is another that first became known in Europe from the collections of the German explorer and natural history collector, J.F. Drège. Most of Drège's plant specimens were entrusted to Professor Ernst Meyer, of Konigsberg (now Kaliningrad), for description, but he, in turn, sent the orchid specimens to Lindley, who was then Professor of Botany at University College, London. Lindley described this species in the genus *Bonatea* and gave it the epithet *clavata* in allusion to the elongated stigmatic arms which are enlarged in the form of a club at their extreme tip. Reichenbach transferred this species to the genus *Habenaria* in 1865.

Habenaria is a very large genus with over six hundred species in a worldwide distribution; approximately one-third of these occur in Africa. There is tremendous variation in size within the genus, but most species have green flowers; a few have some white parts and yellow is also present rather rarely. The name *Habenaria* comes from the Latin word *habena* (reins), and was coined by the German botanist Willdenow in allusion to the long, strap-shaped divisions of the petals and lip. Of the thirty species that are recorded in South Africa, *Habenaria clavata* has the largest flowers, but in the tropical parts of the continent there are others with larger or much more striking flowers. Some of the East African species in the section *Multipartitae*, in which the flowers are large and the lateral lobes of the lip are variously fringed, are very spectacular. In the majority of species, however, the flowers are small and, in the wild, the inflorescences are hard to see in the surrounding green vegetation.

Species of *Habenaria* are encountered in many different vegetation types, ranging from rain forest to swamps and from lush, damp, grasslands to stony hillsides. With their underground tubers, they are very well-suited to withstand a prolonged period when conditions may be too hot or too cold but are certainly too dry for normal growth. Consequently, many species put forth new shoots with the onset of rainy conditions in early summer and flower when the rains are well-advanced. Only a few flower early in the spring after extremely rapid growth.

Habenaria clavata is a grassland species that is widespread in Africa. In the west it has been collected in northern Nigeria, and from there its range extends across to Ethiopia. Though curiously absent from Kenya, apparently, it has been collected in Tanzania and Zaïre and thence southwards as far as Transkei and the eastern Cape Province of South Africa.

PLATE 4
Bonatea lamprophylla

A handsome terrestrial herb reaching 100 cm or more in height. Underground it has several elongated tubers as well as extensive roots. A new stem arises every spring, bearing two or three sheaths at the base and ten to fourteen beautifully shining leaves with crispate margins. Near the flowers the leaves decrease in size and the green bracts of the inflorescence resemble them on a still smaller scale. The inflorescence is pyramidal in shape, bearing six to thirteen elegant flowers. They stand, stiff and proud, apart from the supporting stem, each one with a detailed and striking arrangement of its parts. The sepals are green: the dorsal one is erect and concave and nearly 4 cm long; the laterals are paler green, deflexed below the lip and somewhat twisted. Each petal has two distinct lobes: the upper one is green and adherent to the front margin of the dorsal sepal while the lower is horn-shaped, linear or curved, and yellowish-white in colour. Beyond its narrow whitish base the lip has three narrow lobes. The middle lobe is green, 5 cm long, and wider than the slender, flexuous side lobes, which are paler green and 13–16 cm long. The darker green spur is 11–12 cm long and conspicuously swollen and flattened in its apical part. Enclosed in the hood of the dorsal sepal lie the two bright yellow pollinia of the single anther. Their long slender caudicles rest on the upper surface of the side lobes of the rostellum and the bright brown viscidium of each one is visible at the tip of these slender lobes. The rostellum also has a bright green, hooded, central lobe with a pair of yellowish-green staminodes alongside the base of its outer margin. Below it, and resting on the lip, is the pair of stigmatic lobes which have a creamy-coloured receptive surface.   *Plant x1/10; inflorescence x3/4*

Bonatea lamprophylla J. Stewart in *American Orchid Society Bulletin*, **47**: 992–997 (1978)

This is the largest species in the small genus *Bonatea* and it is remarkable that it escaped collection and description until very recently. It differs from the well-known and widespread *B. steudneri* by its even greater size, its attractive leaves, and several features of the flowers: the petals, with their stiff, forward-pointing lower lobes are particularly striking and the lip is also different in the extreme length of its long, narrow side lobes. As a genus, *Bonatea* is distinguished from *Habenaria* by the curiously large and three-lobed rostellum that stands in front of the anther, by the fact that all the lower parts of the flower — the lateral sepals, lower petal lobe, lip base and stigmatic arms — are partially united near their base, and by the presence of an elongated tooth-like structure in the mouth of the spur.

The specimen illustrated was presented to the author in 1976 by Barbara Jeppe, who had collected it in dune forest not far from the sea, at Mabebe in northern Natal. It was growing in deep shade, in almost pure sand, and was easily recognised as distinct, even in the bud stage, from the smaller-flowered *B. speciosa*, which grew in the same area. The broad leaves have a crispate, wavy margin and a lustrous, shining surface that looks as if it has been polished. Hence, the specific epiphet was derived from the Greek words *lamprus*: shining or radiant, and *phylla*: leaves.

In cultivation it has proved quite easy, and the leafy spike is present on the plant for most of the year. Thirteen flowers were produced in 1977, closely arranged to present a green and white mop-like inflorescence, while the wild-collected specimens bore six and ten flowers each. Flowering appears to occur regularly in October, so that this would be a good time to search for it in the other shady patches of dune forest and scrub that still exist along the coasts of Natal and Mozambique.

PLATE 5
Bartholina burmanniana

A dwarf terrestrial plant, which reappears each spring from a small spherical tuber. The solitary leaf is almost circular in outline; it clasps the flowering stem quite firmly and is often somewhat raised above the surface of the sandy soil because of its convex shape. The large flowers are always solitary at the apex of a slender scape that is densely clothed with long, spreading hairs. The light green sepals stand up in a row at the back of the open flower. The pale violet petals, which sometimes have darker violet markings, are upright, too, and in face view they fit neatly into the gaps between the sepals. The fan-shaped lip with its numerous filiform segments extends from 4–8 cm in diameter and is the most conspicuous feature of the flower. Its pale mauve fringe is demarcated from the pale green central area by a violet border. At the base of the lip a greenish spur extends backwards below the curved ovary. *Plants life size*

Bartholina burmanniana (Linnaeus) Ker in *Journal of Science and the Arts*, **4**: 204, t. 6, figure 2 (1818)
Orchis burmanniana Linnaeus, *Plantae Rariores Africanae*, 26 (1761)

This extraordinary orchid holds several distinctions. It was one of the first African orchids to be properly described in Europe and one of the few that were seen and named by Carolus Linnaeus, the Swedish 'father of modern botany'. In 1760–61 he described a collection of plants loaned to him by the Dutch physician and botanist, Johannes Burman. He named this species in honour of Burman, without giving any information about the actual specimen, its origin or collector. Fifty years later the same species was described, under another name, in the new genus, *Bartholina*, by Robert Brown, the English botanist who was then Sir Joseph Banks's librarian.

The name *Bartholina* commemorates a famous Dane, Thomas Bartholin, who was born in 1616 and became Professor, first of Mathematics and later of Anatomy, at Copenhagen. He was himself the son of an eminent anatomist, and in due course his five sons all became professors, of Anatomy, Antiquities, Theology, Mathematics and History, respectively.

The quaint but dramatic flowers of this curious orchid led early colonists of South Africa, who were accustomed to associate orchid flowers with insects and other animals, to refer to it as the 'spider orchid'. A second species was described by the famous Cape orchidologist, Harry Bolus, in 1884: *Bartholina etheliae*, in which the segments of the lip are expanded and globose at the tip, was named for his daughter, Ethel, who often helped her father with his work, and 'who first detected the plants hidden under bushes'. Both species of *Bartholina* occur in grassland and in stony places among heaths and other fine-leaved bushes. They are somewhat uncommon and are found only in the Cape Province of South Africa, mostly in the south.

They are not difficult to flower in cultivation, at least in the first year after their introduction from the wild, but maintaining the plants is much less easy. The first living plants seen in flower in Europe, in 1787, were introduced to the Royal Botanic Gardens, Kew, from the collections of Francis Masson, the energetic Scottish gardener who was the first collector to be sent abroad, officially, from Kew, on the advice of Sir Joseph Banks. Further tubers were sent to Kew in 1892, by Harry Bolus, and they flowered there in the following July, at the same time of year that the species normally flowers in South Africa. The plants illustrated in the accompanying plate were presented to the author by Frieda Duckitt, of Darling, who has kept a large collection of Cape orchids in cultivation for many years.

E.J.Hennessy

PLATE 6
Huttonaea grandiflora

A modest terrestrial species with intricate and intriguing flowers. The slender flowering stem bears two sessile leaves near its base, both of them ovate or cordate, glabrous and rather pale green. The flowers are white, cream or palest green and every part of them is curiously fringed. The dorsal sepal is small and erect, almost hidden behind the petals, while the lateral sepals are much broader and spreading. The two petals stand erect behind the column. They are united in the narrow basal part and diverge above it into broadly triangular limbs. At the base of each limb there is a fairly shallow sac, or spur, with a number of papillae occluding its lower edge. The limb of each petal falls forward to shade the column or sometimes stands erect, exposing it clearly to view. Their edges are deeply fringed with tiny papillose appendages, as is the lower edge of the broad, radiate lip. On the short, broad column the diverging anther cells, with their coarsely granular pollinia, are very obvious.   *Plants life size*

Huttonaea grandiflora (Schlechter) Rolfe in Thiselton-Dyer (editor), *Flora Capensis*, 5(3): 114 (1912)
Huttonaea oreophila Schlechter var. *grandiflora* Schlechter in Engler, *Botanische Jahrbucher*, 24: 420 (1898)

This attractive and unusual plant represents a small genus of only five species of South African orchids that are more or less confined to the Drakensberg mountain range and its outliers. All the species are immediately recognisable by the fringed outer edge of the petals and lip, but they have diversified to fill a number of different ecological niches. The type species, *Huttonaea pulchra*, grows in the shadiest parts of the forest floor, and like the smaller-flowered species, *H. fimbriata*, it waits until summer is well-advanced before putting forth leaves and flowering stems. Two more species, *H. woodii* and *H. oreophila*, are grassland plants, although the latter is often found in rocky situations, as its name implies. The species chosen for illustration has the largest flowers in the genus and is found at the highest altitudes. It occurs on grassy ledges and in moist places on mountainsides, more than 2500 metres above sea level. These plants came from slopes near Sani Pass, in the south of Natal, where a rough road climbs over the lip of the escarpment into Lesotho. They were growing in very moist, shallow soil overlying basaltic rocks. Elsewhere, plants have also been collected at the northern end of the Natal Drakensberg, near Witsieshoek, the type locality for this distinctive species.

Rather few orchid genera have been named in honour of female orchid collectors. *Huttonaea*, as the spelling of its name suggests, was dedicated to Mrs Henry Hutton, who travelled with her husband, a magistrate, and collected a number of botanical specimens in the eastern Cape Province in the middle of the nineteenth century. She sent her material to William Henry Harvey, the Irish botanist, who had lived at the Cape for six years before retiring to Dublin where he became Curator of the herbarium at Trinity College. His botanical exploits began while he was Treasurer-General of the Cape Colony, and, as he noted in his diary: 'I mean to occupy my leisure in preparing for my *Flora Capensis* which I find is a book very much wanted, and one which requires to be written on the spot'. Before he died, in 1866, he completed the third volume of this monumental work. The account of the orchids was prepared by the Kew botanist, Robert Allen Rolfe, and published in 1912–13; the whole work was not finished until 1933 and it has never been superseded. Although he did not live to see *Flora Capensis* completed, Harvey also published two volumes of his *Thesaurus Capensis*, in which specimens of South African plants, selected from the Dublin herbarium, were illustrated and briefly described. The second of these appeared in 1863 and contained a drawing of Mrs Hutton's specimen, as its first illustration, to accompany the description of her genus.

PLATE 7
Disa crassicornis

A terrestrial plant with a stout flowering stem up to 50 cm long. The stem is rather sparsely leafy and a separate leafy shoot, bearing two or three leaves that are longer and wider than those on the stem, arises next to it. The stem leaves are oblong or oblong-lanceolate with acute tips, up to 13 cm long and 3 cm wide. On the upper part of the stem the leaves become smaller and gradually merge into the bracts. At flowering time most of the leaves are already rather shrivelled and brown, and the bracts are papery and rusty-red. Five to ten flowers take up half the length of the stem. They are always pink, variously spotted with a dark wine red, and very sweeetly scented. The dorsal sepal is distinctly oblong when seen from the front but triangular in side view and gradually contracting into the slender greenish spur, which is 3–4 cm long. The lateral sepals are broader than the petals and lip, the latter being the narrowest of the perianth parts. The stigma forms a white sticky boss at the front of the column. It quickly becomes yellow as it receives pollen from visiting insects, after which the flower soon fades.   *Plant x1/6; inflorescence life size*

Disa crassicornis Lindley, *The Genera and Species of Orchidaceous Plants*, 346 (1838)
Disa jacottetiae Kraenzlin in *Vierteljahrsschrift der Naturforschenden Gesellschaft in Zurich*, **60**: 391 (1915)

This elegant species has been collected in a wide range of habitats and localities in southern Africa. It has been recorded on various isolated mountains in several parts of Cape Province, Natal, Lesotho and Transkei, and from near the sea up to an altitude of 2600 metres. The type specimen, used by Lindley in the first description of the species, was collected by the German explorer J.F. Drège, high up in the Witteberg Range of the eastern Cape mountains. It proves to be very similar to the plant illustrated here, which was collected near Witsieshoek, at the northern end of the Natal Drakensberg, at a very similar altitude.

In his description of *Disa jacottetiae*, in 1915, the German orchidologist, Fritz Kraenzlin, admitted that the specimen collected by Hélène Jacottet, and for whom it was named, was reminiscent of *D. crassicornis* Lindley, but he thought it could be distinguished from it by its different flower colour and by characters of the spur and the dorsal sepal which he did not elaborate. Mademoiselle Jacottet was an adventurous person who travelled with her brother, Dr Lautré Jacottet, a medical missionary, to many remote parts of Lesotho during the years 1905 to 1914. She collected plants in several high mountain areas that have rarely been visited by botanists either before or since. It seems a pity that this attractive disa will no longer commemorate her activities, but recent studies of a wide range of specimens indicate that Kraenzlin was mistaken in thinking that her specimen was distinct from *D. crassicornis*. The name *D. jacottetiae* must be regarded, henceforth, as a synonym.

Because of its attractive, gladiolus-like flowers, this species has been collected and brought into cultivation rather frequently. It has been grown successfully, from time to time, but is not easy to maintain for a long period. It was reported in cultivation in Europe as early as 1879, at the Glasnevin Botanic Gardens. Probably the best chance of success would be to treat this species as a temperate garden plant. The seasonal changes it experiences in the wild range from intermittent snow cover in winter to high temperatures and storms of tropical intensity in summer. If suitable cultural conditions permit growth and flowering, the fragrance of this delightful species will add to its visual attraction in any orchid collection.

E. J. Hennessy

PLATE 8
Disa sagittalis

A small terrestrial or lithophytic plant with a rosette of glaucous green leaves that arises annually above a conical tuber. The leaves are spreading and have sinuous, undulate margins. The stout, erect stem is rather short and surrounded by a number of membranous sheaths. The flowers are medium-sized and very striking, white or pale mauve in colour, often with streaks of a much darker colour in the scintillating surface of the sepals and petals. The dorsal sepal is most unusual: it is broad at the base with a short tapering spur behind the column; then, for about 1 cm of its length, it stands erect before dividing into two rounded lobes which project backwards almost at a right angle from the rest of the sepal. The lateral sepals extend forward, below the base of the column, in the same plane as the lobes of the dorsal sepal but in the opposite direction. The linear petals are also erect, in front of the dorsal sepal, and each has a broad basal lobe which overlaps the base of the short linear lip. The column is held horizontally within the flower but is almost hidden by the enclosing petals and lip.   *Plants life size*

Disa sagittalis (Linnaeus *filius*) Swartz in *Kongliga Vetenskaps Academiens Nya Handlingar*, **21**: 212 (1800)
Orchis sagittalis Linnaeus *filius, Supplementum Plantarum*, 399 (1781)

The flowers of the genus *Disa* are extremely varied; the four species illustrated in this book demonstrate only a fraction of the details that can be found in more than one hundred species that have been described so far. In all the species, the dorsal sepal is uppermost and bears some kind of spur or sac at its hooded apex. But it appears to have acquired the propensity displayed by the lip in many other orchid genera, to exhibit distinctive, even extravagant features. In *D. sagittalis*, the dorsal sepal gives the flower a very odd, almost eared appearance, which is extremely difficult to interpret in a dried specimen. Nevertheless these details were faithfully recorded, in Latin, by the younger Linnaeus, when he first described this species. He also noticed the arrow-shaped tips of the two petals, which stand erect in front of the dorsal sepal, and to which the epithet *sagittalis* refers.

Andreas Sparrman collected the type specimen of *Disa sagittalis*. He had been one of Linnaeus's pupils, and arrived in Cape Town in 1772, four days before his friend and colleague, Thunberg. They botanised together on the lower slopes of Table Mountain on several different excursions, but after only a few months Sparrman sent all his botanical specimens back to Linnaeus and joined Captain James Cook on his second voyage round the world. He returned to the Cape in 1775 and towards the end of the year began a long journey eastwards, through the forests of the Knysna area, eventually reaching the summer rainfall region of South Africa. He was always most enthusiastic about the plants he collected, especially during spring in the Cape. He once recorded: 'The pleasure of a botanist who finds all at once so rich a collection of unknown, rare and beautiful vernal flowers in so unfrequented a part of the world is easier to be conceived than described'. Many orchids were among his finds. All were sent back to Sweden, where some were described by the younger Linnaeus. The task of completing the descriptions of all the orchid specimens that had accumulated at Uppsala, from the activities of both Sparrman and Thunberg, was carried out by another Swedish botanist, Olof Swartz, in 1800.

This species is nearly always found growing amongst rocks, on ledges between successive blocks of sandstone, in the deeper soil that accumulates amongst boulders and in the narrow chinks and cracks that sometimes form across rock faces. Its distribution in South Africa is entirely eastern and it extends from the southern, coastal borders of Natal, through Transkei, down to the eastern and southern areas of Cape Province.

PLATE 9
Disa tripetaloides

A tough terrestrial plant of marshy or stream-side situations. The plants propagate themselves underground by creeping rhizomes, which arise from the axils of the lowermost leaves. Each cluster of leaves arises from a bud on the rhizome where thick fleshy roots also develop. The long, somewhat glaucous and shiny leaves are mostly radical but a few ascend the stem, becoming gradually smaller until the bracts appear. Their light green colour contrasts strangely with the dull red of the flowering stem. Up to twenty flowers are borne in a somewhat lax raceme. The flowers are 2–3 cm in diameter, white tinged with pink, and more or less dotted with rose-purple. The dorsal sepal is decidedly bonnet-shaped and has a short conical, greenish spur. The lateral sepals are proportionately large while the tiny petals, lip and column are hard to distinguish in the very centre of the flower. Following pollination, the lateral sepals fold up and hide them completely, and soon the whole flower turns reddish-brown as the tiny ovary develops into a fat brown capsule containing thousands of seeds.   *Plants life size*

Disa tripetaloides (Linnaeus *filius*) N.E. Brown in *The Gardener's Chronicle 1889*, 360 (1889)
Orchis tripetaloides Linnaeus *filius, Supplementum Plantarum*, 398 (1781)

This attractive yet modest species was first collected by the Swedish botanist Carl Peter Thunberg and described by the younger Linnaeus, who classified it in the genus *Orchis*. Over a hundred years passed before the Kew botanist N.E. Brown transferred it to *Disa*. The species came to his attention as a living plant in the collection of James O'Brien at Harrow, who recommended it to orchid collectors. 'It is not only the freest growing and most profuse flowering *Disa* I ever saw,' he wrote to Brown 'but also the most easily grown of South African terrestrial orchids . . . . It lasts in flower a wonderful time, and would be a very prolific plant to grow for cut flowers . . . . It is like an elegant, small example of *Disa crassicornis*, white spotted with red; an exquisitely pretty species.'

It is, perhaps, not surprising that this species proved so easy to cultivate in England. In the wild it is found in Cape Province, a little east of Cape Town, and occurs in many places around the south-eastern coast of the continent as far as the southermost corner of Natal. It is a plant of stream banks and other damp places and is often found growing among true *Sphagnum* mosses and other bog-loving plants. Although found in frost-free areas, it does not require great heat and plants spread and increase easily by means of their underground stolons. The plant illustrated here was collected near Port Edward, and grown in the collection of Ron and Terry Slater of Queensburgh in Natal.

Soon after it was brought into cultivation in England, this species was successfully hybridised with the much more difficult *Disa uniflora*. A very attractive pink-flowered hybrid, which was intermediate between the parents in size, was raised at Kew and named Kewensis. Other hybrids were raised from it and the two parents, and named in due course, including Elwesii, Premier and Watsonii. None of these attractive orchids has been seen in cultivation for many years, but several growers in the Cape Province of South Africa have recreated and are trying to raise them. The most exciting prospect comes from the use as a parent of the bright yellow variety *aurata*, instead of the white and pink form of *Disa tripetaloides*. This variety was recently re-collected from the southern slopes of the Langeberg mountains where it was first discovered by the English explorer, William Burchell, in 1815. Harry Bolus re-collected it there seventy-five years later and, in 1977, a party led by Professor E.A. Schelpe of Cape Town found it again; on this occasion plants were brought into cultivation for the first time.

E.F.Hennessy

PLATE 10
Disa uniflora

A spectacular terrestrial orchid whose flowering shoots crown a swollen tuber and many roots. Often, new growths will arise around a parent plant from axillary shoots which spread underground. Each shoot bears five to eight linear-lanceolate leaves, which are stiffly or laxly held to form a basal rosette for the stem. They are sheathing at the base, often somewhat ribbed along the surface and acuminate at the tip. The upper leaves are smaller and resemble the bracts, and in the upper part of the stem a single bract supports each flower. Two to four flowers are usually borne on each plant, but there may be only one or as many as eight or ten, each one being 8–12 cm in diameter. The large dorsal sepal is slightly hooded and bears a spur, little more than 1 cm long, near its base; its inner surface is a yellowish-cream, sometimes rosy-tinted, and bears a number of red, solid and broken veins. The lateral sepals are usually plain orange red, scarlet or crimson in colour, and each is more than 5 cm long. The petals are smaller and stand behind the central anther; each is as red or redder than the sepals on the outer surface but bright yellow and dotted with red on the more conspicuous inner surface. The relatively small lip projects forward between the lateral sepals. A pure white-flowered form was collected many years ago and a yellow form, entirely lacking any red pigment, was discovered recently. In all these flowers, the white central column is surmounted by two linear anther cells which each contain an elongated pollinium; the shiny boss of the sticky stigma is separated from them by the broad white rostellum.

Plants life size

Disa uniflora Bergius, *Descriptiones plantarum ex Capite Bonae Spei*, 348, t. 4, f. 7 (1767)
Disa grandiflora Linnaeus *filius, Supplementum Plantarum*, 406 (1781)

The genus *Disa* was established by the Swedish physician and botanist, P.J. Bergius, when he described the species illustrated here, but he never explained how he derived the generic name. Several possible explanations have been discussed, and the most likely seems to be that it is an allusion to the beauty and magnificence of the flower (from the Latin, *dis*, rich or opulent). The red disa is so spectacular that it has been known for a long time as the 'Pride of Table Mountain'. It was once very common on Cape Town's conspicuous backdrop, and is now also known in several other montane habitats in South Africa. Several writers have been more expansive: it has been referred to as 'the most superbly magnificent of all Orchids' and as 'Queen of terrestrial orchids'. For the southern hemisphere, at least, the latter seems an appropriate accolade.

The English botanist, John Ray, first described the red disa, in 1704, as '*Orchis africana flore singulari herbaceo*'. However, the correct name of a flowering plant is the first name properly published for it after 1753, when Linnaeus's book, *Species Plantarum*, appeared. Thus the somewhat inappropriate name, *Disa uniflora*, which Bergius proposed fourteen years before the epithet *grandiflora* was published by Linnaeus's son, will always be the correct name for this species.

This disa is also remarkable in being one of the few orchids of Africa that have been used in a programme of hybridisation. The first hybrid, *Disa* Veitchii, was made with another Cape species, *D. racemosa*, and flowered in England at the nursery of James Veitch and Sons in 1891. Many subsequent crossings involving these two species and their progeny led to the production of hybrids called Diores, Luna, Blackii, Julia K. Stockley and Italia, as well as others in which *Disa tripetaloides* was the second parent.

In the wild, *D. uniflora* grows in a wide variety of situations: in black peaty soil and in almost white sand, under the drips of waterfalls or high up on stream banks, with its roots in fast-flowing streams, among rocks, or intertwined with those of reeds and other stream-side plants. It can be found at sea level and up to 2000 metres above, in full sunlight, or in very shady places. Clearly, it is a very adaptable species and, provided it can be kept free of fungus and bacterial infection, will give its growers enormous pleasure.

E. F. Hennessy

PLATE 11
Brownleea macroceras

A slender terrestrial herb with a simple underground tuber. The delicate stem supports a single, narrowly lanceolate leaf, which has a long acuminate tip. The leaf is usually held erect but may be spreading or recurved. Altogether the flowering stem reaches 15–18 cm high and bears only one to three flowers. Each arises in the axil of a green bract, which clasps the stem and is similar to the leaf but smaller. The medium-sized flowers are a delicate pale mauve or blue but fade to white as they age. The dorsal sepal is uppermost and a little more than 1 cm high. It extends backwards into a cylindrical greenish spur that is slightly bulbous at its tip and more than 3 cm long. The lateral sepals spread outwards and downwards away from the column, making, with the erect dorsal sepal, a neat triangular shape when the flower is viewed from the front. The petals are also lanceolate but they cohere with the outer margin of the dorsal sepal, providing it with a distinctive border, and are difficult to distinguish at first sight. Similarly the lip, which is extremely small, is erect, spurless, and only just visible as a darker flap across the base of the white column. *Plants life size*

Brownleea macroceras Sonder in *Linnaea*, **19**: 106 (1847)
Brownleea monophylla Schlechter in Engler, *Botanische Jahrbucher 20*, Beiblatt **50**: 8 (1895)

The small genus *Brownleea* is closely related to *Disa* but is distinguished from it by the petals, which are always more or less united to the margin of the dorsal sepal, and by the lip, which is always very small, often curved upwards and held very close to the front of the column. The name of the genus was suggested to the English orchidologist, John Lindley, by the Irish botanist, Harvey, in honour of the collector of two different species near King William's Town, in South Africa. John Brownlee was a Scottish missionary who first collected both *B. coerulea*, the type species, and *B. parviflora* in damp shady places not far from his mission on the Buffalo river. The first of these is now known to be widespread in South Africa while the second extends northwards as far as Kenya in the east and Cameroun in the west. Recent studies indicate that six species of *Brownleea* are now known to occur in Africa.

The species illustrated here has the largest flowers in the genus and the most delightful. Only a few flowers are borne on elegant, graceful stems that are supported by the wiry mountain grasses and sedges among which these small plants hide. The specific epithet was chosen, presumably, to describe the long spur (from the Greek: *makros*, long or large; *keras*, horn) that is carried by the dorsal sepal. The species was first collected on the Katberg mountains of the eastern Cape by the German botanist and traveller Carl Zeyher, a professional plant collector, who later settled in Cape Town. It has since been found at various sites along the Drakensberg mountain range, always at rather high altitudes. The plants used for the painting were collected at the northern end of the Natal Drakensberg, near Witsieshoek, and not far from the locality where Justus Thode, an itinerant tutor and amateur botanist, collected the type specimen of *B. monophylla*. Recent comparative studies have shown that Rudolf Schlechter was wrong to describe this specimen as a new species and it merely represents a fine form of *B. macroceras*.

This plant must be grown as an alpine. In the wild it experiences warm wet summers and cold dry winters but the tubers are buried many centimetres below the surface of the soil and are well protected from frost. Like many other 'afro-alpines' it is very welcome in cultivation and should not prove any more difficult than the high altitude plants of Europe and Asia that are so highly prized.

PLATE 12
Herschelia baurii

A slender herbaceous terrestrial, with very narrow grass-like leaves arising from an underground tuber. Even the newest leaves are somewhat brown and shrivelled at flowering time and at its base each plant is surrounded by the thread-like, fibrous remains of leaves from previous years. In comparison with the leaves, the scapes, 20–30 cm in length, appear almost stout. Each bears several narrow sheaths and three to eight flowers. The flowers are variable in size and in overall colour, from almost pink, through various shades of mauve to a true, almost caerulean blue. The dorsal sepal is galeate and extends backwards into a greenish spur of varying length, sometimes as much as 10 mm long. The lateral sepals extend forwards and sideways and are often paler in colour. The petals are almost hidden inside the dorsal sepal. They are very small and lobed, but conspicuous by their bright green and purple coloration. The purple lip with its fringed border is a very attractive feature of the flower.

Plants life size

Herschelia baurii (Bolus) Kraenzlin, *Orchidacearum Genera et Species*, **1**: 804 (1901)
Disa baurii Bolus in *Journal of the Linnean Society*, **25**: 174, figure 12 (1889)

The English orchidologist, John Lindley, established the genus *Herschelia* in honour of Sir John Herschel, who spent the years 1834 to 1838 in Cape Town and found time to collect, study and illustrate some of the wild flowers while conducting his famous astronomical survey. Since then the genus has been regarded as a section of the genus *Disa* by several botanists and retained as a distinct genus closely related to *Disa* by others. In *Disa*, two slender pollinia are borne on separate caudicles each with its own viscidium, whereas in *Herschelia* the pollinia share a single viscidium and are much rounder. In the latter genus nearly all the species have blue or blue-tinged flowers and a large, often conspicuously fringed or lobed lip. They all display a rather fragile habit and have narrow, grass-like leaves. Altogether these characters seem sufficiently distinctive to validate the retention of Lindley's name. He first proposed it for the brilliantly blue Cape species, *H. coelestis* (now regarded as a synonym of *H. graminifolia*), and particularly appropriately, for he described this superb species as having 'the most beautiful colour of the intensely blue southern sky': while the generic name commemorates the astronomer, the specific epithet referred to the heavens.

The wiry spikes of *Herschelia baurii* appear every year from August to November, rather early in the growing season of the southern hemisphere, while the surrounding grasslands are still sere and brown from the frosts of winter, or as they bear a flush of short green growth following their denudation by fire. Few other flowers are available to foraging insects at this time and almost every flower attracts visitors. Examination of a colony of plants on the slopes of Natal's Drakensberg mountains one year revealed that every flower, except those which obviously had opened only on that day, had been pollinated. Many bore the evidence of bright yellow massulae of pollen grains on the white stigma, while in others the perianth was already drooping as the ovary swelled. The strategy of flowering while there is little competition for pollinators is clearly successful.

This species was named in honour of Leopold Baur, a pharmacist, botanical collector and Moravian missionary, who collected it one February during the period (1862–75) when he lived near Bazeia mountain, now part of Transkei. The flowering season seems unusual, compared with what we now know of this species, but it is quite likely that the plant gathered by Baur was stimulated into growth and flowering at this time by a summer fire. Hailstorms and untimely fires promote out of season flowering in many South African cormous and bulbous plants. This species is now known to be widespread in Natal and parts of the Transvaal in a wide range of undisturbed grassland habitats, at altitudes from sea level to 2000 metres.

E. J. Hennessy

PLATE 13
Satyrium carneum

A robust and stately terrestrial orchid with a stiff, almost succulent habit. Two large leaves appear above the underground tuber and lie flat on the surface of the ground; each one is ovate, or sometimes nearly orbicular, and often more than 20 cm long. The stout flowering stem appears between these leaves and is embraced by several smaller leaves which give way to pale green bracts that are crossed with reticulate pinkish-red veins. The large pink flowers are borne in a dense cluster at the apex of the stem, among the very wide bracts, on which they appear to rest as they open. The sepals and petals are united to the lip near its base and are all rather similar, thick and fleshy, with a slight keel on the outer surface and a pointed tip. The lip is borne on the upper side of the flower and the twin spurs at its base lie alongside the ovary with their tips tucked into the bract. The free part of the lip is helmet-shaped, with a keel along its upper surface ending before a conspicuous pointed flap that is reflexed slightly to reveal the tip of the long slender column. *Plant x1/2; inflorescence x3/4*

Satyrium carneum (Aiton) R. Brown in Aiton *filius, Hortus Kewensis* ed. 2, **5:** 196 (1813)
Orchis carnea Aiton, *Hortus Kewensis* ed. 1, **3:** 294 (1789)

This species of *Satyrium* is one of the largest in South Africa. The inflorescence is shown at almost its natural size but the complete plant has been considerably reduced. The plant portrayed was presented to the author by Frieda Duckitt, of Darling, who has mastered the art of cultivating and propagating this demanding genus. By strict adherence to the normal rainfall regime of the western Cape district, which has a Mediterranean climate with mild, wet winters and hot, dry summers, this plant has been maintained in good health for several years. A rising mound, in the centre of the sandy compost in which it grows, is usually the first sign that new leaves are about to appear, after the long dry period. Once they have emerged, they grow rapidly and spread flat over the surface. Careful watering is necessary to ensure that they are not damaged.

After a few months the stout flowering spike emerges between the leaves. Its flowers are a delicate pink and white, the colour of an English complexion, which may have suggested the epithet *carnea* (fleshy) to Jonas Dryander, who was Sir Joseph Banks's librarian. One of his tasks was assisting William Aiton, then chief gardener at Kew, in the production of a catalogue, which was an annotated list of what was growing in the Royal Botanic Garden at Kew. Dryander probably wrote the botanical description of *Orchis carnea* for Aiton. Plants were grown from tubers sent back to Kew by the Scottish gardener-collector, Francis Masson. When the second, enlarged edition of the *Hortus Kewensis* was being prepared by Aiton's son, Robert Brown, who had succeeded Dryander at Banks's house, prepared the botanical descriptions. It was therefore Brown who suggested the transfer of this species to its proper place in *Satyrium*, a genus that Olof Swartz had established in 1800.

Only a few terrestrial orchids from Africa have been grown or propagated successfully in other lands, but at the beginning of the nineteenth century this *Satyrium* was reported to be flowering in the collection of Mr Griffin, at South Lambeth in England. At this time, 1812, it was illustrated in the important periodical established by William Curtis, then known as *The Botanical Magazine*, and in the description that accompanied the illustration, John Sims, who edited the magazine, referred to this species as the 'Great-flowered Cape *Satyrium*'. It was the first African orchid to be included in the magazine, which was started in 1787 and is still published regularly today.

PLATE 14
Satyrium coriifolium

A striking terrestrial orchid with brilliant flowers on its stiff, straight spike. This plant is 20-60 cm high and carries three to five leaves at the base of the upright stem. The lowermost leaf is small, embracing the stem, and the next two are the largest, oval in shape and fleshy in texture. All the leaves, and the bracts that ascend the stem, are conspicuously spotted or barred with maroon on the lower surface. The spike is dense and bears many flowers of flame-coloured hues; they may be yellow, deep orange or almost red and as each emerges above its bract the latter bends suddenly back, almost as if it were broken. The flowers are held horizontally with the entrance to the column facing the ground. The hooded lip is uppermost and more brightly coloured than the other perianth lobes. From its base two short but slender spurs descend on either side of the ovary, while the front border of the lip appears slightly three-lobed with the paler side lobes dependent and the smaller middle lobe recurved upwards at its tip. Below the lip the lateral sepals stand out like wings, while the slightly narrower petals and third sepal are all dependent. At their base all these parts are united for a short distance. *Plant x3/4*

Satyrium coriifolium Swartz in *Kongliga Vetenskaps Academiens Nya Handlingar*, **21**: 212 (1800)

The second of the two Cape species of *Satyrium* that have been selected for this book is very brightly coloured, common in the wild, and quite unmistakable. Its fiery spikes stand out brightly from the dull, greyish-green leaves of the heaths and other low, fine-leaved bushes amongst which it frequently grows. It is one of the commonest orchid species growing in and around Cape Town, and huge bowls of cut spikes are still displayed at the spring wildflower shows in many parts of the south-western Cape.

This species was one of the first plants that were collected in Africa as botanical specimens. In the second half of the seventeenth century, a young physician, Paul Hermann, was employed by the Dutch East India Company to practise in Ceylon. On his journey there in 1672, and on his way back to Holland in 1680, he botanised at the Cape and took his plant specimens home with him. He died at Leiden in 1695, but part of his herbarium collection of Cape plants was acquired by William Sherard at Oxford University. At some stage these were loaned to the English botanist, John Ray, and he included a description of this species in the third volume of his *Historia Plantarum*, in 1704. The specimen of *S. coriifolium*, annotated in Ray's handwriting, is still preserved in the Sherard Herbarium at Oxford.

An illustration of this species was published in 1729, by J. C. Buxbaum, in Russia. Although most of his illustrations were rather vague, this one is easily recognisable and well described in the caption '*Orchis lutea caule purpureo maculato*' (a yellow orchid with purple dotted stem). It seems likely that this published illustration was based on a painting made by an artist at the Cape, and although the original has not as yet been located, it is of particular interest in that it is the first, known, published illustration of an African orchid.

The flowering period of this species, in the wild, is spread over nearly half the year: early specimens can be collected in July and there are still a few late ones to be found in November. It is fairly widespread in Cape Province, extending eastwards as far as Port Elizabeth where the plant illustrated here was collected by a Swiss botanist, Dr Jany Renz. In the southern Cape it hybridises rather freely with other species of *Satyrium* growing nearby. Mixed populations are known that consist of *S. carneum, S. coriifolium,* and their intermediates, as well as other hybrid swarms in which the second parent is the pink-flowered *S. erectum*. It is, itself, rather variable in colour, and the additional colours provided by the hybrids increase the range of pale, pretty colours that occur among the Cape orchid flowers.

PLATE 15
Satyrium rhodanthum

A rare and beautiful species of exquisite colour and splendid size. The erect straight stems ascend to 25-40 cm in height before the leaves appear from the adjacent bud on the underground tuber. The stems are glabrous and almost entirely covered by closely embracing sheaths. These merge with the bracts, which are erect at first but soon become deflexed as the flowers open. The lower ones are long, much longer than the flowers, but the upper ones become gradually smaller. They are tinged or streaked with the same wine-red colour as the strikingly beautiful flowers. The lip is hooded and somewhat inflated, with an almost square border surrounding the round entrance to the column. At its base the two slender spurs are twice as long as the ovary and they descend below each flower between the bracts. The lateral sepals are wide and wing-like, free almost to the base, and more conspicuous than the similar, but smaller, intermediate sepal and petals.

Plants x4/5 and x1/3

Satyrium rhodanthum Schlechter in Engler, *Botanische Jahrbucher,* **40**: 92 (1908)

The third *Satyrium* we have selected provides a contrast in both growth habit and flower colour to the two previous species. It is also remarkable in that it was discovered relatively recently and is still known from grassy hillsides on only two farms in southern Natal, South Africa.

When the plants illustrated in the painting were collected, in the middle of October, a single leaf had just appeared through the soil surface immediately adjacent to the fully developed flowering stem. A second leaf appeared subsequently in the axil of the first, so that the plant consisted of two shoots, one reproductive and colourful, the other green, vegetative and sterile. Two distinct shoots are produced by a number of species of *Satyrium*, the most well known being the very variable *S. longicauda*. Two other species in South Africa are *S. neglectum*, which has small pink flowers in very long spikes, and the larger-flowered *S. woodii*. The latter is, in fact, rather similar to *S. rhodanthum* but the flowers are differently coloured (pink or pale orange-red), in larger inflorescences, and the leaves are fully developed at the time this species flowers. Further north, in the southern highlands of Tanzania, a number of other species produce their leaves on a separate shoot, adjacent to the flowering stem.

Satyrium is a genus of approximately one hundred species, of which forty are recorded in South Africa and nearly the same number in East Africa. Five species have been reported from Madagascar and two in Asia. All members of this terrestrial genus are immediately recognisable by the fact that the lip is held on the upper side of the flower and that it usually bears two tubular spurs, symmetrically, at its base. The sepals and petals are united to form the margin of the lower side of the flower and provide a landing platform for the insect pollinator.

Brilliant colours are characteristic of *Satyrium* flowers and are the major pollinator-attractant, but in *S. rhodanthum* they are more vivid than in any other species the author has seen. In many East African species the flowers are a beautiful rose pink, bright yellow, orange-red, or deep carmine, but none has the deep, rich colour of *S. rhodanthum*, a colour enhanced by the velvety texture of the perianth and shiny surface of the bracts. The epithet *rhodanthum*, red-flowered, is entirely appropriate for this species.

PLATE 16
Disperis capensis

Two forms of this slender terrestrial species are illustrated together in order to portray their similarities and differences. The slender erect stems are rather hairy in the lower part and bear only a single leaf, or two, about halfway along their length. One or two flowers are borne near the apex of the stem. The flowers are the largest in the genus and basically yellowish-green in colour, although the petals of the commoner form are a brilliant rose purple. The dorsal sepal is bluntly hooded and bears a long tubular appendage extending upwards from its front edge. The lateral sepals are free and completely reflexed, each with an obtuse sac or spur near the base, and ending in a narrowly acuminate tip. The petals are held close to the dorsal sepal along one margin but differ from it by their colour and are not difficult to detach. The complex lip is folded back over the column and bears a curiously toothed and papillose appendage on its face, but almost the whole of the lip is hidden inside the dorsal sepal. *Plants life size*

Disperis capensis (Linnaeus *filius*) Swartz in *Kongliga Vetenskaps Academiens Nya Handlingar*, **21**: 218 (1800)
Arethusa capensis Linnaeus *filius*, *Supplementum Plantarum*, 405 (1781)

The genus *Disperis* is an easy one to recognise by its saccate, or spurred, lateral sepals, to which the name refers (from the Greek, *dis*: twice, and *pera*: sac or pouch). It was named by the Swedish botanist Olof Swartz when he dealt with all the orchid specimens that had accumulated at Uppsala after Linnaeus's death, and reclassified some species that had already been named by Linnaeus's son.

Most of the species of *Disperis* are found in the Afro-Malagasy region, but a few representatives are found as far afield as Java, New Guinea, Thailand, Taiwan and the Philippines. Several of the African species are widely distributed in the tropical regions but in the south of South Africa, where the climatic regime is markedly different from that of the rest of the continent, there is a small group of species of more restricted range. Of these, the one which has the largest flowers is one of four that were described by Swartz in 1800, *D. capensis*.

This species is remarkable for the long slender tips that terminate all its sepals. In the green-flowered form, the flowers appear heavier and tougher and the sepals are wider at the base. These plants differ, too, in being generally more robust than the slender and elegant plants with rose-purple petals, and by their much more hairy stems. Although illustrated together on the opposite page, they do not grow together in the wild: the greenish forms are always found on steep slopes, in short turf growing in shallow, stony soil, and have been recorded in only a few places in the southern Cape Province; the purple-petalled plants occur in marshy places or are sheltered among heaths and other low-growing bushes, and are widespread from the Cape Peninsula to Algoa Bay. They are one of the largest and most conspicuous among the winter-flowering orchids.

The first specimen collected, on which Linnaeus's son based his original description, was sent to Sweden by Carl Peter Thunberg, who probably found it on the Cape Peninsula. He was one of Linnaeus's most brilliant pupils, and had been invited to collect plants in Japan for some of the leading horticulturists of Holland. He arrived at the Cape in 1772 and stayed there for three years, partly in order to collect plants, but also to become familiar with the Dutch language, without which he would have been unable to travel in Japan. He collected assiduously in South Africa, and joined the Kew gardener Francis Masson in two long journeys from Cape Town to the hinterland. Before he eventually left for Japan, his notes and a very large number of botanical specimens were sent back to Uppsala. Because of these travels, collections and later contributions to the study of the country's flora, Thunberg is often described as the 'father of South African botany'.

E. F. Hennessy

PLATE 17
Disperis fanniniae

A slender, glabrous terrestrial of delicate appearance and fragile habit. Plants vary in height from very few to more than 40 cm tall. Several leaves are borne on the erect stem, each of them lanceolate but cordate and clasping the stem at its base. The bracts are leaf-like in shape and form, and each supports a large, white flower that is often tinged with purple. The dorsal sepal is deeply hooded, or bonnet-shaped, while the saccate lateral sepals are lanceolate with narrow, pointed tips. The petals are stuck to the dorsal sepal along the inner margin, but each has a prominent rounded lobe along the outer margin that is often spotted with green or purple and provides a pretty 'frill' to the 'bonnet'. The linear lip is folded back over the column into the hood of the dorsal sepal and its narrow but bilobed appendage is minutely papillose.

Plants x4/5

Disperis fanniniae Harvey, *Thesaurus Capensis*, **2**: 46, t. 171 (1863)

The common name, 'Granny's Bonnet', is applied to several different species of South African orchids. In the species of *Disperis* illustrated here, it is given in allusion to the deeply hooded dorsal sepal, which appears to be perched above a little face that is framed by the decorative petals. Depending on its stage of growth, the centre of the flower may remind the careful observer with a favourable angle of view of a miniature imitation of a human face, albeit with a green nose. The spurred lateral sepals clearly indicate that it is a member of the genus *Disperis*, and when it was described by the Irish botanist William Henry Harvey, he named it in honour of the collector who sent the specimens to him from Natal, Mrs George Fannin. She was the wife of one of the early farmers in the Midlands of Natal and with her husband collected many plants, particularly orchids and asclepiads, for botanical study.

This species is now known over quite a wide area in eastern South Africa, from the eastern Cape Province northwards to the Transvaal. It favours very shady places on the forest floor and is also found in shallow pockets of soil on rocks and sometimes in crevices between boulders and on cliffs. It appears to be equally at home in both the indigenous forests that still remain in the areas of its range and in the pine plantations that have replaced them and covered many areas that were formerly grassland. It is also quite prolific in uncultivated, shady parts of several large gardens that border indigenous forests. A single plant that appeared in the author's garden several years ago has been followed by many others, which have become established, apparently from seed, in the shade of cypress trees. Here they probably share a propitious mycorrhizal association, perhaps with the same fungus that is exploited by the trees and flourishes in the deep leaf litter that has accumulated round their boles.

The leaves are a very attractive feature of these dainty orchids. They have an elegant, pleasing shape and a delightful texture. When illumined in a shaft of sunlight that strikes through the forest canopy they have an almost iridescent quality, and the richness of the gleaming upper surface contrasts bravely with the shining purple below. Plants that develop in better-lit situations have duller leaves in that they appear a darkish-green but are quite ordinary in surface characters.

E. F. Hennessy

PLATE 18
Didymoplexis verrucosa

An extraordinary saprophyte, which appears suddenly above the dead leaves that litter the forest floor from a series of large, colourless tubers that lie just below the surface. The leafless slender stem is pale brown and bears only a few scattered bracts. The delicate flowers are white, tinged with pinkish-brown, and are borne in a terminal raceme, each in the axil of a small pointed bract. While still in bud, the brownish outer surface of the sepals bears conspicuous whitish warts that are still visible in the mature flowers. The flowers open in sequence: usually not more than two are available to pollinators at any time, and each is open for only a few hours. The sepals and petals are united at the base to form a briefly tubular perianth. This surrounds the base of the broad lip, which is three-lobed at its apex. Many bright yellow warty outgrowths, formed by variously shaped papillae, are arranged in a band across the central area of the middle lobe of the lip. The short column is slightly winged on either side near the apex. After pollination, which often occurs without the buds opening, the pedicel elongates at an astonishing rate so that the fruiting capsule is projected 15 cm or more above the apex of the stem.

Plants x4/5

Didymoplexis verrucosa J. Stewart and E.F. Hennessy in *American Orchid Society Bulletin*, **49**: 836–842 (1980)

The discovery of this unusual orchid in the dune forest at Mtunzini in Natal, South Africa, was an exciting event for a visiting botanist, Professor C.G.G.J. van Steenis, and for the landowner, Ian Garland, in November 1975. We visited the site in August 1978, to collect material for illustration and description, and again in February 1980 when there were no signs of plants. In the meantime, an intensive search through the literature at the University of Natal and at Kew had revealed that our plant differed in several conspicuous ways from the specimens described as *D. africana* from Tanzania. The callosities on the lip are somewhat similar to those described in *D. pallens*, an Asiatic species of wide distribution. At first we thought that the Zululand plant fell within the range of variation exhibited by that species. But when other features of the flower were listed, including the fact that it is not clearly resupinate, the lip being held on the upper side of the flowers, the column is short and straight rather than curved, the lip is clearly three-lobed, and the union of the sepals and petals is much less marked than in any of the other species so far described, it became clear that these plants represented another, as yet undescribed species of the intriguing genus, *Didymoplexis*. We named it *D. verrucosa* in allusion to its warty sepals and lip.

The name of the genus is derived from two Greek words, *didymus*, double or twin, and *plexus*, plaited, but Griffith did not explain why he coined this name when he first described the genus in 1844. Perhaps it refers to the two rather meagre wings on either side of the column, or to the double row of yellow papillae that are situated along the midline of the lip in *D. pallens*. One of the most characteristic and extraordinary features of the genus, which was mentioned by Griffith and has been referred to by every botanist who has described any of the species since his time, is the way in which the pedicels elongate rapidly and conspicuously while the fruits are maturing.

In the forest at Mtunzini, this species grows in a layer of soil only 10–15 cm thick. It has been derived from rotting leaf litter and other decaying plant parts, and still contains a large amount of woody material. Underlying the soil is coarse sand, which has been deposited on this aggrading coastline during the last sixty years or so. Although these orchid plants resemble some species of *Striga* that are root parasites, in their absence of chlorophyll, size and coloration, no connections with any of the tree roots that thread their way through the soft forest soil could be discovered. As in all other species of *Didymoplexis*, they are probably saprophytic in nature.

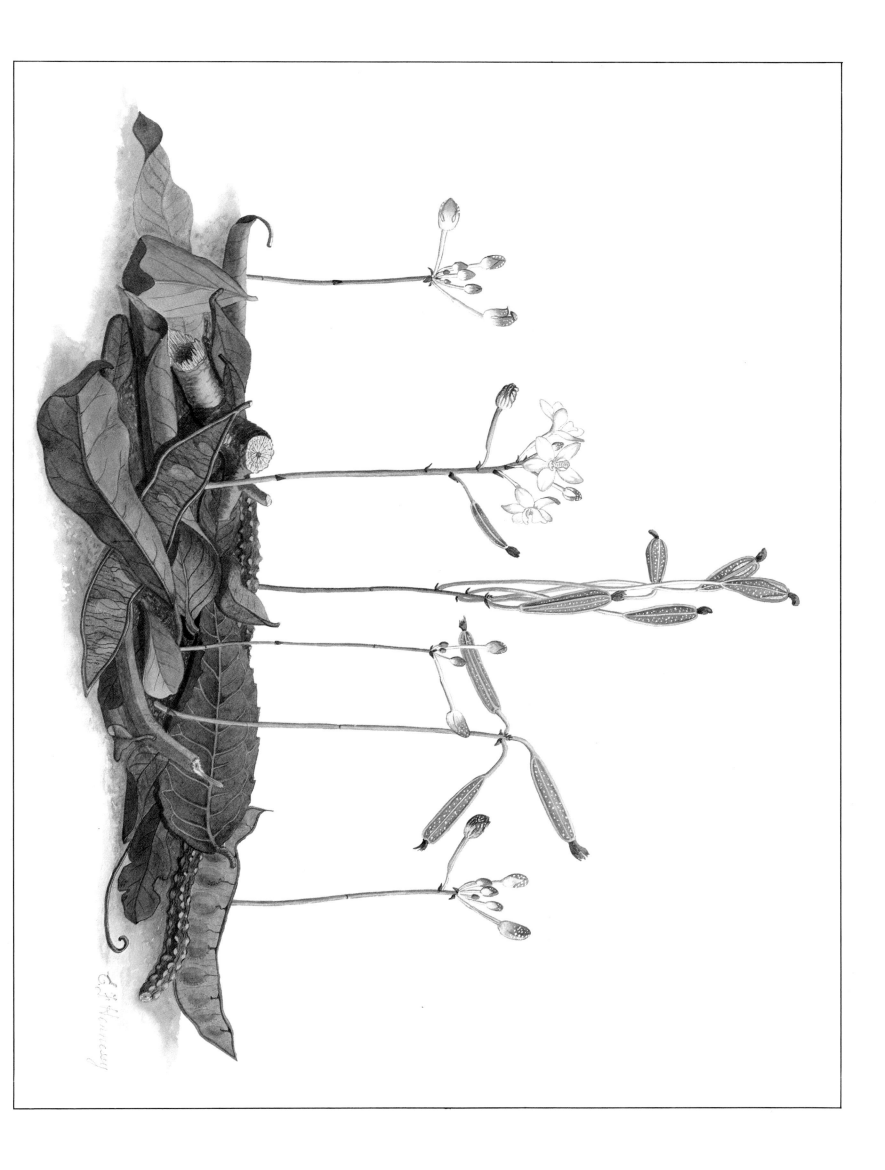

PLATE 19
Ancistrochilus rothschildianus

A tufted epiphyte, with squat, more or less conical pseudobulbs, arising close together from a basal rhizome. Every spring a new pseudobulb expands gradually within the base of the rapidly enlarging leaves of the new shoot. The plicate leaves elongate to 20 cm or more, but by the time they are mature the tips are already beginning to die off. Each leaf is abscissed, some way above each pseudobulb, soon after the growth of the latter is complete. At the same time, the inflorescences arise from the base of the newly completed pseudobulb. The softly hairy peduncle bears two or three flowers that are 5-8 cm in diameter. The sepals are broader than the petals but only slightly longer, and have the same pink coloration. The lip is distinctly three-lobed: the basal lobes are upright, rounded and greenish with brown or mauve markings, while the narrow middle lobe is bright lilac purple and strongly ridged along its upper surface. The robust column is prominent in the centre of each flower and is dark brownish-mauve in colour; it conceals eight pollinia, arranged in pairs, under the moveable, pale-coloured cap at its tip. *Plant life size*

Ancistrochilus rothschildianus O'Brien in *Gardener's Chronicle* series 3, **41**: 51, figure 24 (1907)

*A*ncistrochilus is a small genus of only two species. It was established in 1897 by the English orchidologist, R.A. Rolfe, for the only species known at that time which had already been described as *Pachystoma thomsonianum*. H.G. Reichenbach's description of the latter, in 1879, was based on plants that were growing in the orchid nursery of Messrs Veitch and which had been sent to them by their collector in West Africa, E. Kalbreyer. The latter had found this pretty epiphyte not far from the coast of southern Nigeria, and requested that it should be named in honour of a missionary who was 'a well-known resident of that pestilent coast'. Subsequently, a number of botanists, including Sir Joseph Hooker, were unhappy about the inclusion of this African epiphyte in an otherwise terrestrial genus known only in several parts of Asia. In writing his account of the orchids for the *Flora of Tropical Africa*, Rolfe settled the difficulty by creating a new genus, *Ancistrochilus*: the name refers to the markedly hooked shape of the middle lobe of the lip.

The second species, which is illustrated here, was added to the genus in 1907 by James O'Brien, the Harrow orchid grower, who was secretary of the Royal Horticultural Society's Orchid Committee for many years. He first described it and dedicated it to Baron Rothschild of Tring Park. The differences between the two species are largely of colour and size: *A. thomsonianus* has small, flattish pseudobulbs and its white flowers are 7-10 cm in diameter with a purplish-red lip, whereas *A. rothschildianus* has larger pseudobulbs that are conical in shape; its flowers are only 5-8 cm in diameter, with a pink perianth and a much shorter and less markedly curved, lilac-purple lip.

In the wild, plants of both species are usually found in flower in the period September to December. Despite their removal from the environs of the Equator, they continue to flower at this time of year in cultivation, both in England and in South Africa. The white-flowered species is known only from southern Nigeria and Cameroun, while *A. rothschildianus* has been collected in Guinea, Sierra Leone, Liberia, Ivory Coast, southern Nigeria, Cameroun, Gabon, Zaïre, and in the Budongo forest of Uganda. Plants are located with difficulty, for their onion-shaped pseudobulbs are always found nestling amongst mosses, ferns and liverworts covering the trunks and lower branches of heavily shaded forest trees. There is a lack of seasonality in the habitat: some rain falls in every month and temperatures vary very little.

These equable conditions indicate that no special treatment is necessary in cultivation. This delightful species needs only a well-drained compost and warm and humid surroundings. With little additional attention it will produce an abundance of graceful flowers, on relatively small plants, at a predictable and regular time every year.

E. F. Hennessy

PLATE 20
Bulbophyllum barbigerum

A quaint and curious epiphyte of dwarf and clustered habit. The lens-shaped pseudobulbs arise close together from a branching basal rhizome, each pseudobulb bearing a solitary leaf that is smooth and fleshy. The inflorescences arise from the base of a recently matured pseudobulb, and each bears rather large bracts, one to each flower, which are pale green at the cordate base and tinged with red at the acuminate tip. Twelve to twenty flowers open in succession on each raceme. The three sepals are narrow, pale green at the pointed tips, yellowish-green at the base and dark purplish-brown between. The petals are reduced to minute scales on either side of the column and are often hard to see. The two dark brown horns on the apex of the column are small but more conspicuous than the petals. It is the lip which is the most comic and curious feature of this extraordinary flower. It is long and narrow, yellow-orange near the base and greenish towards the tip. The whole surface bears a felt of hairs that are bright green at the base and purplish-brown, longer and more luxuriant towards the tip where they form two tufted beards, one above and one below the lip. Intermixed with the beard are two further types of longer hairs, one delicate and slender throughout its length and the other also slender but club-shaped at its tip. *Plant x9/10; flower, side view x5, front view x3*

Bulbophyllum barbigerum Lindley in *Edwards's Botanical Register*, **23**: t. 1942 (1837)

The 'bearded *Bulbophyllum*' was well-named by Lindley, for the lip of this strange and intriguing flower is variously bearded in every part. The longer hairs are never still; the faintest breath of air is sufficient to keep them moving. The slender ones move gracefully and slowly, while the heavier ones with glandular tips oscillate much more rapidly once they are set in motion. The lip itself is also mobile, for, like other members of the enormous genus *Bulbophyllum*, it is articulated at its base with the foot of the column, and the joint is very slight and easily disturbed. When one encounters this plant in flower, in the forest or greenhouse, one has to agree with Lindley, who wrote 'that to breathe upon it is sufficient to produce a rocking movement, so conspicuous and protracted, that one is really tempted to believe that there must be something of an animal nature infused into this most unplant-like production'.

The plant Lindley saw was imported into Britain from Sierra Leone by Messrs Conrad Loddiges, who were the first to introduce several African epiphytes to cultivation. The species is now known to exist in several countries in West Africa, and in addition to Sierra Leone it has been collected in Liberia, Ivory Coast, Ghana, Nigeria, Cameroun and Zaïre. The plant used in this illustration was presented to the author by Carmen Coll of Durban, who purchased it from Margaret Ilgenfritz of Michigan, U.S.A.

Bulbophyllum is an enormous genus of more than one thousand species, with a worldwide distribution. It is particularly well represented in New Guinea (569 species recorded in 1978) and there is a large number of species in Madagascar. It was first described by the French traveller, A.A. du Petit-Thouars, who based his description on a small-flowered plant from Réunion, *Bulbophyllum nutans*. The generic name is derived from two Greek words, *bolbos*, bulb and *phyllon*, leaf, in allusion to the fact that the single leaf, or single pair of leaves, always arises from a bulb-like stem or pseudobulb. The pseudobulbs are borne on a creeping rhizome, and are placed at varying intervals along it. The inflorescence is always a simple raceme, arising from the base of a pseudobulb, but it is very varied in appearance, being slender, thickened in various ways, winged, or bearing only a solitary flower. Although they are usually small, the flowers of *Bulbophyllum* are characterised by the mobile lip, which is often very specialized, and by the toothed or winged column with its two pairs of waxy pollinia.

PLATE 21
Bulbophyllum oxypterum

A rampant epiphyte, with sharply angled pseudobulbs arising at intervals along the creeping rhizome. The narrow, branching roots fasten each node securely to the bark of the branch or the trunk of the host tree. Each pseudobulb is 6-10 cm high and bears two leathery leaves at its apex. One or more inflorescences arise from the base of each newly completed growth. The lower part of the inflorescence is terete, and 15-20 cm long, but the upper part, where the flowers are borne, is expanded into a flat, wing-like portion on either side of the midvein. This upper part, or rachis, continues to grow throughout the flowering period and eventually attains a length of about 25 cm, having borne forty to fifty flowers. They open in succession, each one lasting only a few days. The flowers are very small and the details of shape and colouring are seen best when highly magnified. The lateral sepals are broad at the base, with conspicuous stripes, while the dorsal sepal is narrow throughout its length and tinged with brown or orange on the inner side of its pointed tip. The spotted lip has a hairy margin and is delicately hinged at its base. The shape of the narrow petals is copied, in miniature, by the curving stelidia borne on the apex of the column on either side of its bright yellow tip.   *Plant x4/5; flower and bud x10*

Bulbophyllum oxypterum (Lindley) Reichenbach *filius* in Walpers, *Annales botanices systematicae*, **6**: 258 (1861)
Megaclinium oxypterum Lindley in *Edwards's Botanical Register*, 25, misc. 14 (1839)

This widespread species of *Bulbophyllum* is a representative of a section of the genus called *Megaclinium*, which is confined to Africa. The sectional name describes the flower-bearing portion of the inflorescence, which is extended sideways into a wing on either side of the rachis and in which the flowers often appear to be embedded (from the Greek *mega*, wide and *kline*, bed). The section was originally treated as a separate genus, by Lindley, who proposed it in 1830, but because its growth habit and flower structure are basically so similar to other species of *Bulbophyllum* it has long been regarded as merely a section of that genus.

The species on which Lindley based the genus *Megaclinium* came from Sierra Leone, but representatives of this section are now known to be widely distributed. *Bulbophyllum oxypterum* occurs in West Africa and also from Kenya southwards to Mozambique and Zimbabwe on the eastern side of the continent. It seems to be very closely related to *Bulbophyllum maximum*, which is found only in West Africa, and can be distinguished from it by several characters of the rachis and flowers. In *B. oxypterum*, the rachis is somewhat narrower, has smooth, flat margins that are never undulate, and is unevenly expanded so that the flowers are borne nearer to one margin instead of centrally. When the tiny flowers are enlarged it is easy to distinguish the long, acuminate dorsal sepal, and the curved lip, whose apex is tucked tightly away out of sight.

The yellowish-green colour of the pseudobulbs and leaves indicates that this species grows in strong light, almost fully exposed to the sun in the canopy of forest trees. In cultivation, the plant has grown well near the roof of a fibreglass greenhouse and has maintained its natural colour. The plant illustrated was presented to the author by Klasie van der Merwe of Pietermaritzburg, who obtained it from Zimbabwe.

PLATE 22
Cirrhopetalum umbellatum

A creeping epiphyte, with pseudobulbs arising at intervals along a fibre-covered rhizome, which also bears narrow wiry roots. The pseudobulbs are conical in shape with a green, ribbed or sharply angled surface. Each is surrounded by the fibrous remains of an encasing sheath and surmounted by a single leathery leaf. The slender-stalked inflorescences arise one at a time, successively, over quite a long period, from the base of each pseudobulb. Each wiry stem bears an umbel of five to eight flowers which develop, and open, simultaneously. The colouring of the flowers is very variable. Basically it is pale yellow or pinkish, overlaid with pink or red, and frequently spotted, but very pale and very dark forms are known, as well as some that are almost red or maroon and others that are nearly yellow. The dorsal sepal is almost hemispherical and bears a long vibratile antenna at its tip. The lateral sepals, 2.5–4 cm long, are individually twisted so that the outer surface of each lies uppermost and then the outer edges are fused together for more than half their length, leaving a small gap near the base through which the lip can move. The narrow petals have fringed edges and each bears an antenna slightly shorter than that on the dorsal sepal. The small, curved, shiny lip is articulated at its base and can move backwards through the gap in the lateral sepals or forwards to fill the space between it and the curved column. Two long, narrow stelidia project forward from the apex of the column, adding further to the spiky appearance of each flower. *Plant life size*

Cirrhopetalum umbellatum (Forster *filius*) Hooker and Arnott in *The botany of Captain Beechey's Voyage*, 71 (1832)
Epidendrum umbellatum Forster *filius*, *Florulae insularum australium Prodromus*, 60 (1786)
Bulbophyllum longiflorum Thouars, *Histoire particulière des plantes orchidées recueillies sur les trois iles australes d'Afrique, de France, de Bourbon et de Madagascar*, t. 98 (1822)
Cirrhopetalum thouarsii Lindley in *The Botanical Register*, **10**: t. 832 (1824)
Cirrhopetalum longiflorum (Thouars) Schlechter in *Beihefte zum Botanisches Centralblatt*, **33**(2): 420 (1915)
Cirrhopetalum africanum Schlechter in Engler, *Botanische Jahrbucher*, **53**: 573 (1915)

The list of synonyms given above is by no means a complete one for this attractive species, but it indicates the variety of names that have been used for it in the African region. It became known from Madagascar and the other islands of the western Indian Ocean long before it was discovered in Uganda and Tanzania on the mainland of Africa. Perhaps not surprisingly, plants were collected recently in the north east of Natal, adding another genus to the known orchid flora of South Africa. Studies carried out not long ago among the worldwide collection of orchid specimens in the herbarium at the Royal Botanic Gardens, Kew, revealed that these African plants should be allocated to the same species as one collected by the Forsters, father and son, in the South Pacific, during their passage with Captain James Cook in his second voyage round the world.

To complicate the situation somewhat further, some botanists consider that the genus *Cirrhopetalum* cannot be recognised as clearly distinct from *Bulbophyllum*. This species looks different enough, with its umbellate inflorescence, enormously enlarged and partially united lateral sepals, and the long tail-like fringing hairs on its petals, but in Asia there are several specimens that cannot be allocated easily to one genus or the other. In both genera, the lip of the flowers is delicately hinged and many species are carrion-scented. Many of the species of *Cirrhopetalum* are very attractive, partly on account of the shape and size of their flowers, but also because of the arrangement of these flowers into an umbel which is sometimes so well displayed that it, in turn, simulates a single large flower.

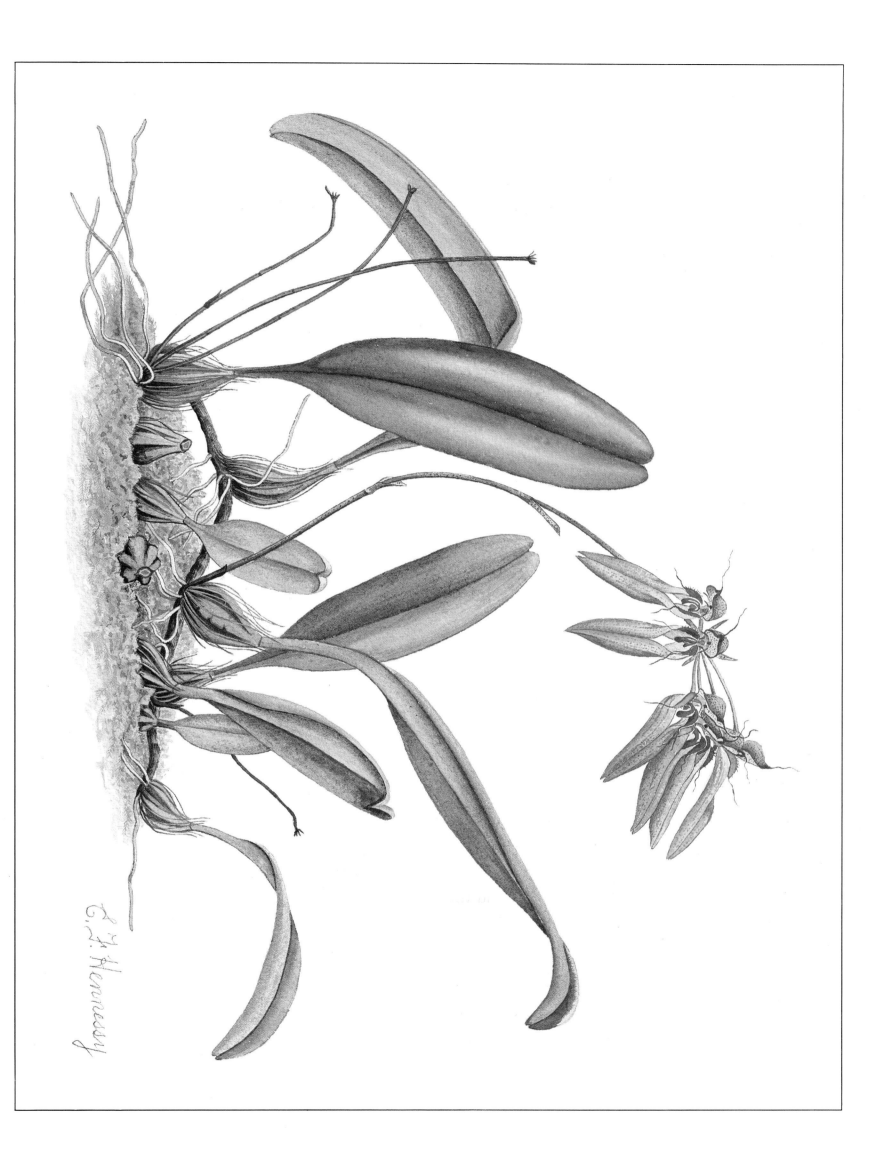

E. F. Hennessy

PLATE 23
Angraecum conchiferum

A delicate epiphyte, with slender branching stems and greyish roots that have an attractive verrucose surface. The leaves arise alternately along the stem and are always linear, less than 1 cm wide, and have an unequally bilobed tip. The slender inflorescences are borne at the nodes, sometimes in the axils of the leaves but more often on the older part of the stem from which the leaves have fallen. Each one bears a single flower, or, occasionally, two flowers. The tepals are gracefully curved and pale green, 2.5–3.5 cm long, though the petals are usually a little shorter than the sepals. The lip is white and shell-shaped, 1.5 cm in diameter, and it always appears on the upper side of the flower because the ovary is twisted through 360°. From the base of the lip the spur hangs vertically downwards and tapers gradually to its pointed tip. The column is short and thick and on the sides of its lower surface two triangular wings project above the entrance to the spur.

Plant x4/5

Angraecum conchiferum Lindley in Hooker, *Companion to the Botanical Magazine*, **2:** 205 (1837)
Angraecum verrucosum Rendle in *Journal of Botany*, **33:** 250 (1895)

In the flowers of all the two hundred or more species of *Angraecum* the lip is concave. It forms a deep cavity around the foot of the column, and extends basally into a spur of varying length. The front part of the lip is very variable in shape and has been described as boat- or shell-shaped in many species. In *A. conchiferum*, the specific epithet means 'shell-bearing' which refers to the shape of the lip and the way in which it appears to be carried in the upper half of the open flower. In the bud stage, this beautiful lip is tightly wrapped within the pale green perianth.

This delicate, slender species was first described from specimens collected in its southernmost habitat, in the Knysna district of South Africa, where it grows in the moist, temperate forests that are not far above sea level. Further north, in Natal, it is found in forests inland, not at a very high altitude, but never near the sea. As one proceeds even further north in Africa, through the Transvaal, Zimbabwe, Mozambique, Malawi and Tanzania it is found only in the cooler, montane forests, and at an ever-increasing altitude until the Equator is reached, in Kenya, and there, on Mount Kenya, it is found only above 2300 metres. The plants grow to considerable size on the shaded branches of forest trees, sometimes covering them completely to make a thick cat's cradle of stems and roots. In September and October, when the flowers are borne, this mass of plants is beset with blossoms that delight the eye, perfume the evening air, and are frequently pollinated. In many parts of its range, the production of capsules from every flower of this species is very frequent.

This is the smallest member, on the African mainland, of the section *Arachnangraecum*, the so-called 'spider angraecums' of which there are very many more species in Madagascar. The leaves are appreciably smaller and usually much narrower than any of the other species. Whilst the flowers are also somewhat smaller, the inflorescences are frequently two-flowered. Most species in the section bear only one flower, on rather short peduncles, at each node along their elongated stems.

No difficulties are presented by this species in cultivation, provided the grower remembers that its native habitat is cool for the greater part of the year and that there is often a pronounced, cooler, dry period. Rainfall is often heavy during the warmer part of the year but is restricted to heavy storms. There are also many periods of continuous misty conditions, when low clouds shroud the trees for several days and all the epiphytes revel in the abundant atmospheric moisture. The specimen illustrated here was collected in the Ngome forest of northern Natal by two botanist colleagues, Olive Hilliard and Bill Burtt, and has grown easily and well in cultivation for several years.

E.F.Hennessy

PLATE 24
Angraecum cultriforme

A small but tough epiphyte which often grows in tangled masses of stems held together by the numerous twisted roots. The stems are short and bear two rows of alternating leaves. Each one is spotted with dark brown and has two sharply pointed lobes at its tip. Roots and inflorescences are borne at the nodes, above the sheath of the leaf they oppose. The inflorescences are described as intervallate, since several arise in succession from the same node. They are thin and wiry and bear up to four flowers in succession before they die. The flowers are a pale salmon-pink or pale green flushed with pink. The sepals and petals are very similar, rather more than 1 cm long, and narrow and pointed. The lip is somewhat concave, lanceolate-ovate, and is sometimes described as boat-shaped. It bears a single raised keel along its surface towards the base and an almost straight spur that is 15 to 26 mm long and noticeably inflated in its apical third.

Plants life size

Angraecum cultriforme Summerhayes in *Kew Bulletin*, **13**: 272 (1958)

In contrast to *A. conchiferum* on the previous plate, this intriguing species of *Angraecum* occurs always at low altitudes, in woodlands and forests that provide only intermittent shade. Temperatures are warm to hot throughout most of the year and the insolation is often intense. In a warm greenhouse it grows easily and its pale pink or greenish-bronze flowers are produced almost continuously throughout the year.

Two plants are illustrated on the accompanying plate. The lower illustration shows a plant collected on Taru Hill in south-east Kenya, by John Lavranos, who presented it to the author in 1975. The bronze tinge that the leaves display is typical of this species in its tropical habitats. The upper illustration shows a plant collected near the southern end of the range of this species, in the forest surrounding Lake St Lucia in Natal, South Africa. In this locality the leaves are rarely so attractive, but their pale, almost dull, green colour is sometimes yellowish or brownish, particularly during the winter months when the shading trees are leafless and the epiphytes receive more sunlight.

This species has become known and appreciated only in the last forty years. It has been recognised in many of the countries between Kenya and Natal, along the eastern side of Africa. It seems very similar to *Angraecum stolzii*, which was first described from southern Tanzania by Rudolf Schlechter in honour of the missionary Adolph Stolz, who collected many interesting specimens while he lived near Mount Rungwe, north of Lake Nyasa (now known as Lake Malawi), between 1899 and 1913. *Angraecum cultriforme* is said to have longer stems, with larger flowers that have longer spurs, than *A. stolzii*, but these are all features of size that can be dependent solely on local growing conditions. The area in which the two species occur is rather similar and detailed studies of more material may show that they are not really distinct. If that proves to be the case, the name *Angraecum stolzii* is the older and must be resurrected for this species.

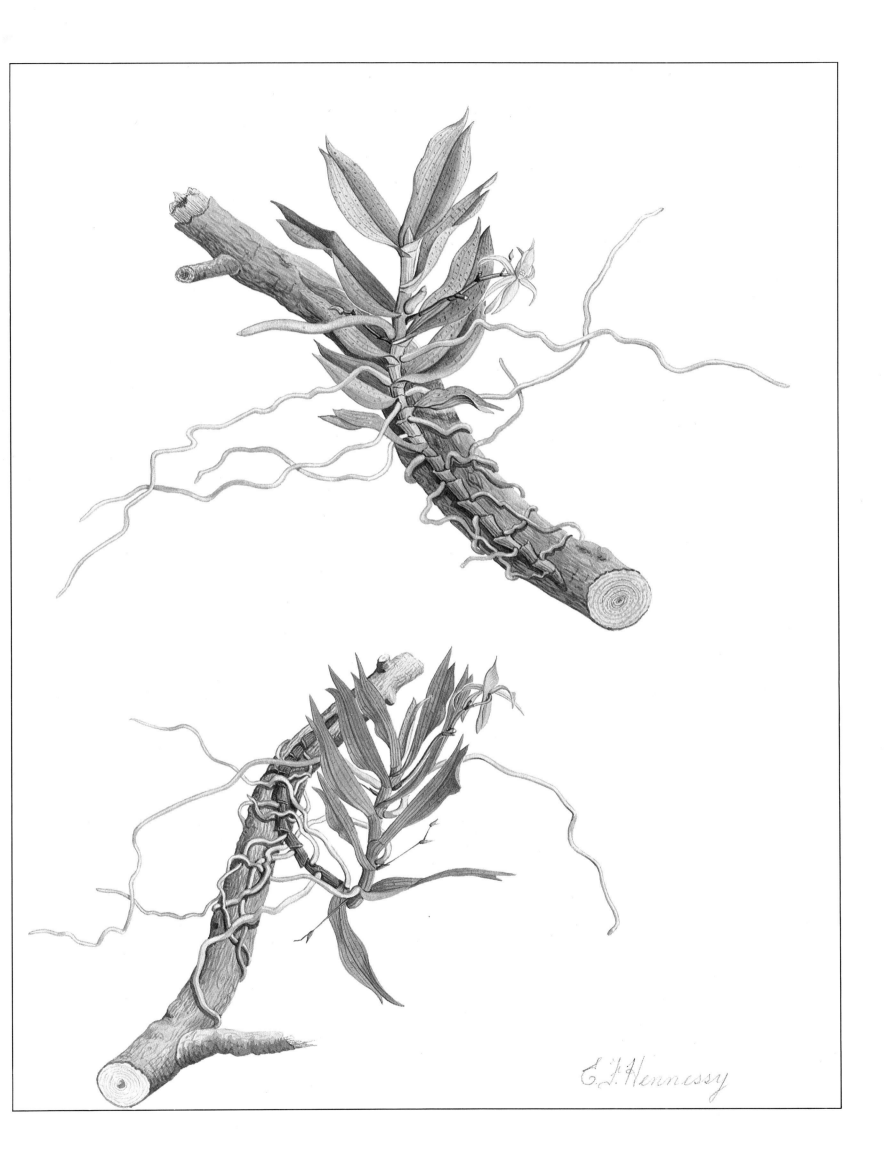

E.F. Hennessy

PLATE 25
Angraecum eburneum subspecies *giryamae*

A robust, epiphytic or epilithic orchid, with stout stems, up to 1 m long, which often bear several 'keikis' near the base so that each plant consists of a large clump of stems. The strap-shaped leaves, up to 60 cm long and 9 cm wide, are borne in two ranks. Each leaf is sharply keeled by the emergent midrib on its lower surface and although it is often leathery, rather than succulent, it maintains a fresh, light green colour. At its tip each leaf is conspicuously bilobed and the lobes are rounded in outline and of unequal length. Many pencil-thick roots emerge from the lower part of the stem, both below and among the sheathing bases of the leaves. Several racemes are usually produced at one flowering season, each bearing ten to twenty green and white flowers in two rows. A triangular brown bract subtends each flower whose ovary is so twisted around the spur of the lip that the latter appears on the upper side of the flowers. The apple-green sepals are 3–4 cm long and the glistening white lip is 3–3.5 cm long and 4–5 cm wide. The lip is apiculate at its apex, and near its base it bears a dart-shaped keel or callus pointing towards the spur opening. The straight spur is 4–6 cm long.   *Plant x1/4; flowers x4/5*

Angraecum eburneum Bory ssp. *giryamae* (Rendle) Cribb and Senghas in *Die Orchidee,* **30**(1): cxxi–cxxii (1979)
Angraecum giryamae Rendle in *Journal of the Linnean Society,* **30**: 388 (1895)

This is a large orchid, perhaps the largest, in plant size, on the African continent. There is no doubt that the size and bulk which even quite a small plant, like the one illustrated here, will attain after a few years in cultivation prevent many orchid-enthusiasts from growing this species. Those who are prepared to accommodate it are amply rewarded in winter with many long-lasting flowers that are sweetly scented every evening.

This subspecies of the well-known *A. eburneum* was described from specimens collected by the Reverend W. E. Taylor of the Church Missionary Society in the Giryama and Shimba hills, near the Kenya coast, in 1887. Since then it has been found in many other localities, often near the shore, frequently scrambling over small rocky cliffs derived from coral, and occasionally as an epiphyte of tall forest trees. Its known range extends from the islands of Zanzibar and Pemba, to the nearby mainland of Tanzania and northwards as far as Kilifi creek in Kenya. In inland districts, it has been recorded in the Usambara mountains of Tanzania by Sir John Kirk in 1887, and at 1800 m on Mount Kilimanjaro by Sir Harry Johnston in 1883. More recently, in 1970, Philip Archer found a new station for it, growing on granitic rocks near the summit of Maungu Hill, in south-east Kenya. The latter plants grow very rapidly in cultivation, beside the coastal forms, but have slightly smaller flowers. In all their native habitats these robust plants are subjected to constant air movement, which varies from a fresh sea breeze to very strong winds. Their distribution is only just south of the Equator, so temperatures are fairly high, but there is usually a distinct fall at night. Light, which varies only slightly from a twelve-hour daily period, is always extremely bright, though plants are usually found in a position where they are shaded during the hottest part of the day.

During a recent visit to the island of Réunion, the author was able to study plants of *Angraecum eburneum* in flower, in the type locality on lava cliffs at the north-east corner of the island. Although considerably further south, they are extremely similar to the Kenya plants in all respects, and rather different from the plants seen in the Comoro Islands and in several parts of Madagascar that have been allocated recently to other subspecies of *A. eburneum*.

Very little hybridisation has been attempted with the African orchids, but this subspecies has been used successfully at least once. *Angraecum* Orchidglade was registered by Jones and Scully in 1964, as the name of a hybrid raised by them in Florida from *A. giryamae* (as it was then known) crossed with *A. sesquipedale*.

E. F. Hennessy

PLATE 26
Angraecum infundibulare

A large-flowered epiphyte, which forms dense growths of many stems in shady positions on the trunks and lower branches of rain forest trees. The leafy stems are very long, sometimes as much as 1–2 m, and often horizontal or pendent. Greyish roots arise opposite the leaves in the lower part, while towards the apex single-flowered inflorescences arise in a similar position. Each leaf is broad and rather flat and its apex is always unequally bilobed. The inflorescence is slender and rather wiry so the flowers are always pendent. The flowers are greenish-white, becoming a pale ivory colour with age except near the centre. The sepals and petals are narrow and elongated, 5–8 cm long. The apiculate lip is of similar length but 4–5 cm broad, decidedly concave and with a distinct greenish tinge in its basal half. Its spur has two distinct sections: the upper part is funnel-shaped and narrows gradually to a point of constriction about 5 cm from the mouth; below the constriction it is more or less tubular for a further 15–18 cm. The whole spur is greenish.

Plant x1/10; branch life size

Angraecum infundibulare Lindley in *Journal of the Linnean Society*, **6**: 136 (1862)

This beautiful species was first collected in Nigeria by Charles Barter who was attached to the Niger Expedition of 1857. He collected extensively in several parts of the valley of the river Niger, and among his collections at Kew there are also a number of specimens from the island of Fernando Po. When he collected it, Barter described this species of *Angraecum* as having 'flowers large, white and fragrant'. The flowers are in fact the largest orchid flowers in Africa, and the funnel-shaped spur at the base of the broad, oblong or ovate lip is particularly spectacular. In cultivation, stems of this species are often grown upright, against a log or tree-fern pole which provides a medium for the attachment of the slender roots. We have chosen to illustrate the plant as it often grows in nature where the stems stand horizontally away from the host branch or trunk. The leaves fall forward slightly in two neat rows on either side of the flattened stem, and the flowers hang down below them.

Rain forests in several countries of tropical Africa provide a home for this species. In addition to southern Nigeria, it is now known from Cameroun, the island of Principe in the Gulf of Guinea, from Congo, Zaïre and Uganda, and was recently collected from the only rain-forest patch remaining in western Kenya. Throughout its natural range the temperatures are warm to hot with little diurnal change. Humidity is always high and in two parts of Uganda where the author has collected this species, near Lake Victoria and in the Budongo Forest, there was surface water in the form of swamp or a river, maintaining the humidity and mosquitoes and adding uncomfortable hazards to the search for this orchid. It has proved easy to grow in cultivation, along with *Phalaenopsis* species and hybrids, enjoying the same conditions of heat, humidity and shade as these tropical Asian plants.

The narrow sepals and petals of this species contrast with the broad, apiculate lip and indicate that it should be classified in the same section of the genus as *A. conchiferum* (Plate 23). The flowers are the largest among the African representatives of the genus, and the spur, which may total 10–18 cm in length, is the longest.

As long ago as 1904, a plant of this species, grown in the collection of Lord Rothschild of Tring Park, received a First Class Certificate from the Royal Horticultural Society in London. This plant had been collected in Uganda, as also were others that were sent to Kew at about this time and which flowered there two years later. The illustration prepared from the Kew plants, published in *Curtis's Botanical Magazine* in 1907, shows a plant trained to grow in an upright position.

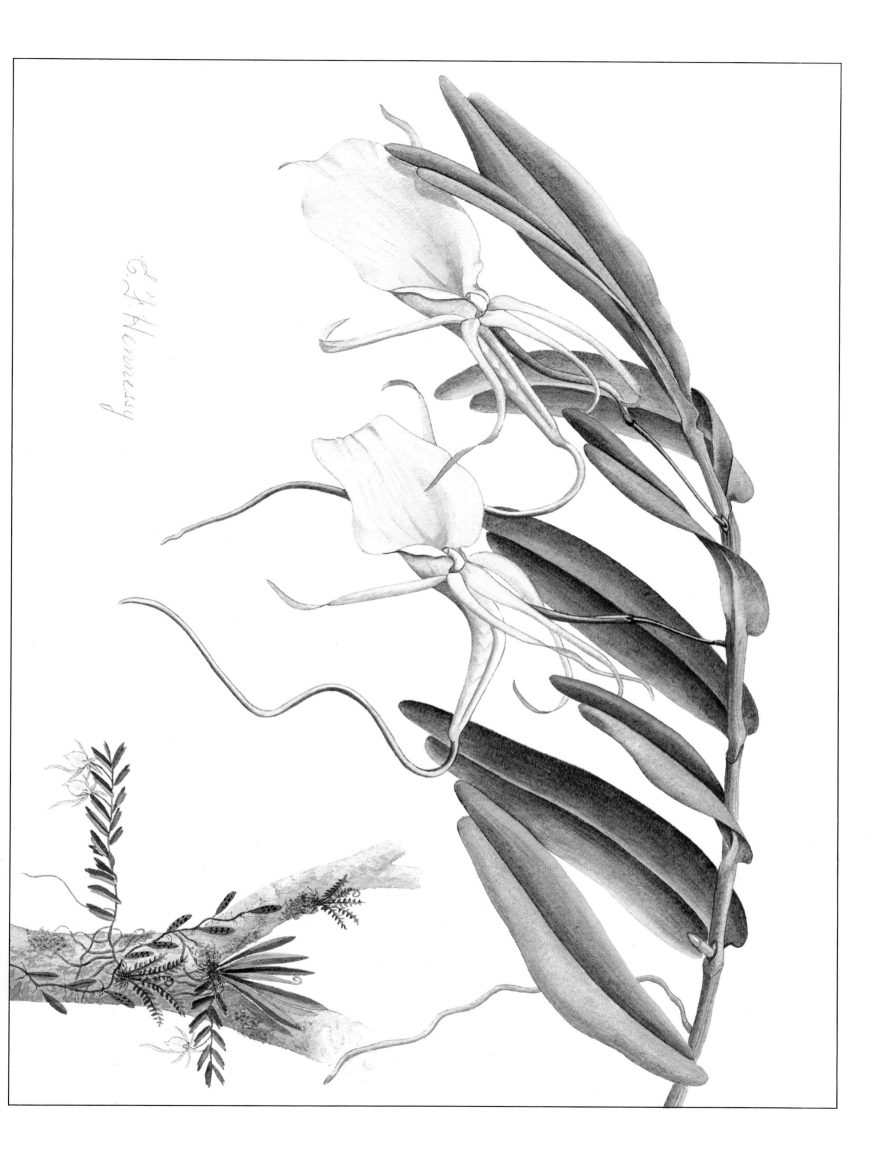

PLATE 27
Angraecum reygaertii

This shade-loving epiphyte has elongated stems , 20–50 cm long, which are flattened rather than round and often pendent except at the tip. The long green leaves are widely spaced on the stem and are always broad, sometimes up to 3.5 cm wide. The inflorescences arise opposite the leaves and although each bears three to five flowers only one is open at any one time. The pedicel of each flower appears to be fused, in its lowest part, with the rachis of the inflorescence, so that the flower arises a little distance above the insertion of its corresponding bract. The flowers are pale green when they first open but quickly turn white, except for a flash on the lip, on either side of the keel, which remains dark green. The tepals are fleshy and 3–4 cm long, the sepals usually longer than the petals. Apart from its central keel the lip is somewhat similar to the petals but bears a wide-mouthed spur at its base. The spur soon becomes narrower and extends for 7–9 cm; it is almost or quite straight and usually pale green.   *Plant life size*

Angraecum reygaertii De Wildeman in *Bulletin du Jardin Botanique de l'État à Bruxelles*, **5**: 190 (1916)

Τhis attractive species seems to be very scarce in cultivation, perhaps because the areas where it grows are so difficult of access, for both geographical and political reasons. The specimen illustrated was collected in western Uganda in 1969. The Bwamba forest, on the north-western slopes of the Ruwenzori mountains, yielded this and several other interesting epiphytes in one brief collecting visit. It appeared to be an epiphyte of slender branches, twigs and lianas that were within a few metres of the ground, rather than in the forest canopy. It was found both near shallow streams that meandered through the humid, shady forest and in areas where the forest floor was swampy from stationary surface water. In cultivation, as in the wild, it requires very shady and warm, humid conditions. It thrives and flowers regularly when grown with species and hybrids of the Asiatic genus *Phalaenopsis*, which have similar requirements.

The specimen on which the Belgian botanist Emile de Wildeman based his description was collected by F. Reygaert, in 1913, at Mobwasa in the north of Zaïre, a little further north and considerably further west than the site from which the author's plant was collected.

This species was chosen as the type of a small group of three African species of *Angraecum*, which were classified together in the section *Afrangraecum* by the late V.S. Summerhayes. All the species have elongated leafy stems, as they also do in the section *Arachnangraecum* illustrated by *A. conchiferum* (Plate 23) and *A. infundibulare* (Plate 26) in this book. But *A. reygaertii* represents a group in which the inflorescences are long and slender and each bears several flowers, although only one flower is usually open at any one time, and sometimes several of the buds fail to develop. All three species are equatorial in distribution and have so far been collected only in Uganda or Zaïre or, in the case of *A. reygaertii*, in both of these countries. This is the largest species of the three, both vegetatively and in the size of its flowers, which are also distinguished by the dark-green coloration near the base of the lip.

E. F. Hennessy

PLATE 28
Diaphananthe pellucida

A very large epiphyte, with robust stems that are at first pendent and then erect, holding the plant well away from the supporting host tree. The thick stem bears large succulent or leathery leaves that can attain 70 cm or more in length and 5–8 cm in width. They are a dark and shiny green, drooping, or gracefully arched away from the stem, and falling in two neat rows to form a most elegant plant. The inflorescences appear in abundance from the lower part of the stem, usually below the leaves, but also in the axils of the lowermost leaves. Five to fifteen long chains of blooms are not at all unusual. Each may bear 40–60 flowers and attain 60–80 cm in length. The flowers themselves are a glistening pearly colour, the edges often tinged with greenish hues or tipped with pale orange brown. The sepals and petals are 9–11 mm long, narrow and acute, while the broad, almost square lip sparkles and appears to be margined with tiny crystalline stars. The short squarish column hides the bright yellow pollinia under a more or less transparent anther cap.   *Plant x2/5; inflorescence life size*

Diaphananthe pellucida (Lindley) Schlechter, *Die Orchidee*, 593 (1914)
Angraecum pellucidum Lindley in *Edwards's Botanical Register*, **30**: t. 2 (1844)

In addition to the magnificent size of the plants and the very elongated inflorescences this species produces, the texture of the flowers is unusual and remarkable. When it was first described and illustrated in 1844, Lindley wrote: 'We lament to see how little justice our artists have been able to do to this beautiful plant, whose flowers are as delicate and transparent as if they were flakes of snow fixed by frost in the very act of melting. Each part of the lip is studded and bordered with little crystalline elevations, and the whole fabric of the blossom is as fragile as thin plates of glass.' Even this poetic panegyric scarcely does justice to the dainty, sparkling flowers.

Although he referred to this species as the 'Transparent *Angraecum*', Lindley was very doubtful that it was correctly placed in that genus, and commented that he wished he had the leisure to undertake a 'reformation in the genus'. It was not until 1914 that the German orchidologist, Rudolf Schlechter, established the genus *Diaphananthe*. He transferred this species to his new genus, as well as a number of other species of African orchids with transparent or diaphanous flowers. They all produce many inflorescences under good growing conditions, both in the wild and in cultivation, but none is quite so spectacular as the species illustrated here.

Lindley's words and accompanying illustration were based on a plant imported from Sierra Leone by Messrs Conrad Loddiges, which flowered in their nursery at Hackney in 1842. The species is now known from all the forested areas of West Africa and extends eastwards in its range as far as Uganda. In the wild it grows on the basal parts of large branches, where there is always a certain amount of shade. The roots spread extensively, but plants are often situated in small deposits of humus, with mosses and other epiphytes. Sometimes they grow on bare bark. The plant illustrated was purchased from Rolf Rawe, who imported it from Ghana.

PLATE 29
Plectrelminthus caudatus

A robust and striking epiphyte with densely leafy stems and very thick greyish roots. The leaves are always borne close together and are light yellowish-green. Each is broadly strap-shaped, 10–35 cm long and 1.5–3.5 cm wide, and unequally two-lobed at the apex. The inflorescences arise in the axils of the lowermost leaves and are usually held horizontally, at least at first, but often become pendent because of the weight of the large fleshy flowers. Four to twelve flowers are borne on the conspicuously zigzag rachis, which is 60 cm or more in length. The flowers are widely spaced, most pleasantly fragrant and long-lasting. The sepals and petals are 3.5–5 cm long and a pale green colour that is often flushed with bronze. The lip is usually upright and is a clear ivory white with its acuminate tip pale green. A curious feature on the basal claw of the lip is formed by two small projections, which make a chevron-shaped bridge that almost unites the two strips of thickened tissue that project forward from the base of the column. The thick, worm-like spur at the base of the claw is 17–25 cm long and spirally twisted. The lateral sepals project backwards behind the spur and are joined together at the base.

Plant x1/5; flowers life size

Plectrelminthus caudatus (Lindley) Summerhayes in *Kew Bulletin 1949*: 441 (1949)
Plectrelminthus bicolor Rafinesque, *Flora Telluriana*, **4**: 42 (1838)
Angraecum caudatum Lindley in *Edwards's Botanical Register,* **22**: t. 1844 (1836)

When this spectacular species first flowered in England, in 1835, it was described as remarkable and extremely rare. The first plants were imported from Sierra Leone by Messrs Conrad Loddiges of Hackney, and were described by Lindley as the 'long-tailed *Angraecum*'. He pointed out the unusual length of the spur, comparing it with *Angraecum sesquipedale* of Madagascar, which has the longest spur that is known. Another feature of the flower that is remarkable is the curious twist at the junction of the pedicel and ovary which causes the flower to be held in such a way that the lip lies parallel with the rachis. Usually the latter is pendent, so that the lip is held in the upright position with the entrance to the spur at its base. When the plant illustrated here flowered, in cultivation, the inflorescence axis remained horizontal.

The large column with its conspicuous anther cap and rostellum are quite extraordinary and unlike any other species in the genus *Angraecum*. Shortly after Lindley's description was published, this species was described again, by the naturalist and author, Constantin Rafinesque, as the type of a new monotypic genus, *Plectrelminthus*. This name refers to the spur being worm-like, and the epithet *bicolor* that Rafinesque used is an appropriate one for this species. Unfortunately Lindley's name was published first so that, although the species is considered to be so different from all others that it must stand in a genus by itself, which correctly bears Rafinesque's name, it must still bear the specific epithet *caudatus*.

Although it is still rare in cultivation, this species is said to be quite common in various parts of West Africa. It is now known throughout a wide belt extending from French Guinea eastwards as far as Gabon and Zaïre. It is always found in areas that are best described as 'warm to hot', and in places where the plants are nearly fully exposed to the strong, direct rays of the equatorial sun. It does not easily produce flowers in cultivation, but grows well near the roof in a warm greenhouse. The best plants the author has seen, with magnificent spikes of blooms, were in the collection of Rolf Rawe, at Kommetjie, in the extreme south of the Cape Province. He very kindly supplied the inflorescence used in the accompanying plate, the author's plants, from Ghana, having refused to flower for a number of years.

PLATE 30
Aerangis brachycarpa

A shade-loving epiphyte, with a mass of greyish aerial roots. The short woody stems may be upright or pendent and they bear four to twelve leaves, alternately arranged, in the upper part. The leaves are dark green, broader above than below, reaching 15–25 cm in length and 2–6 cm in width. The lower surface is paler in colour and is always black-dotted. One or more inflorescences arise from the lower part of the stem. They may be as much as 40 cm long and are always arching or pendent, bearing two to twelve flowers in two distinct rows. On first opening the flowers are pale green, but the tepals turn white as they rapidly expand in size, and sometimes become pinkish as they reflex away from the column. All the tepals are narrow and lanceolate with acuminate tips. On different specimens they vary in length from 20–45 mm, and although the dorsal sepal remains erect the lateral sepals and petals become reflexed within a few days of opening. The deflexed lip bears a slender pendulous spur, 12–20 cm long, which tapers gradually towards a pointed or minutely bifid tip. The column is narrow and terete in its lower part but expands upwards to the side of its broadly oblong stigma and prominent anther.   *Plant x4/5*

Aerangis brachycarpa (A. Richard) Durand and Schinz in *Conspectus Florae Africae*, **5**: 50 (1892)
Dendrobium? brachycarpum A. Richard, *Voyage en Abyssinie*, **5**: 282 (1850)
Aerangis flabellifolia Reichenbach *filius* in *Flora*, **48**: 191 (1865)
Aerangis rohlfsiana (Kraenzlin) Schlechter in *Beihefte zum Botanisches Centralblatt*, 36(2): 120 (1918)

The German orchidologist, H.G. Reichenbach, proposed the genus *Aerangis* in 1865, in a series of publications describing the plants collected in Angola by the Austrian collector Friedrich Welwitsch. At the time, Reichenbach also mentioned specimens that had been collected in Ethiopia, by the German explorer, W.G. Schimper, and apparently realised that they were very similar to the Angolan plants although he retained different names for them. A recently completed study of the genus throughout the continent has revealed that the specimens Reichenbach saw undoubtedly all belong to the same species, which must bear the name *A. brachycarpa*. This epithet was given to the Ethiopian specimens by the French botanist, Achille Richard, in allusion to their elongated, but quite plump fruiting capsules, which bore only the remnants of long-spurred flowers at their upper end. He recorded that the plant was quite unlike any other orchid that he knew: although he tentatively placed it in the genus *Dendrobium*, his published question mark indicates that he was doubtful of its exact generic position.

This species is now known from a wide area in the highland parts of east and central Africa. It occurs between 1500 and 2300 metres above sea level, at higher altitudes near the Equator, in Kenya, Uganda and Tanzania, than in Ethiopia, Zambia and Angola. It is usually found in deep shade, low down on tree trunks and the larger branches of trees, in the forking bases of bushes and sometimes in the cleft of quite thin branches, never far above one's head. The gallery of forest along many African rivers, and the extended patches that surround waterfalls, are favoured sites, but it can be found in many relict areas, even in the small clumps of bushes that frequent termite mounds.

The elongated racemes of slender flowers provide a simple and elegant spectacle in the green dimness of its shady habitat. Towards evening there is the additional excitement of a sweet and heavy perfume that suddenly begins to pervade the air and penetrates to a considerable distance around each plant. As darkness falls the scent becomes even stronger, but it diminishes within a few hours. The performance is repeated daily, throughout the two or three weeks' life of the flower and there is no doubt that this scent, and the abundant supply of nectar in the elongated spur, are special attractions for an, as yet, unidentified moth.

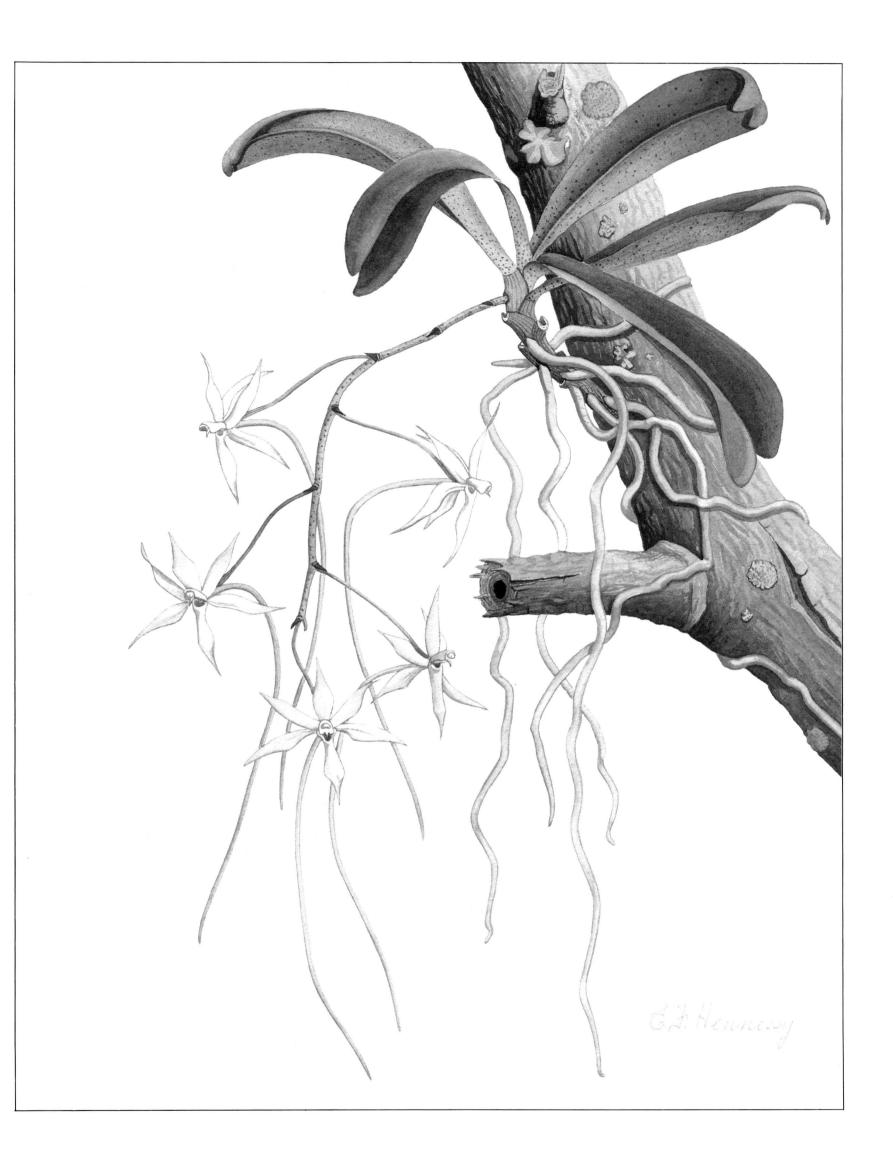

PLATE 31
Aerangis luteo-alba var. *rhodosticta*

A miniature epiphyte with extensive greyish-white roots. Each tiny plant has a very short stem, which is often pendent, bearing two to eight narrow, ligulate leaves. The dark green leaves may reach a length of 15 cm and a width of 15 mm but are often much smaller. The pendent or spreading inflorescences arise below the leaves and bear two to twenty-five flowers in the upper half or two-thirds. This part, the rachis, is slightly zigzag; the dainty flowers are thus positioned in two neat rows, and have their surfaces aligned in one plane. Each flower is 2–3 cm in diameter, flat, symmetrical, and either white or creamy yellow in colour. The petals are a little longer and broader than the sepals. The lip is the largest tepal, being often 20 mm long and 15 mm across at its widest point. Its slender spur is only 2.5–4 cm long, and the copious nectar in its slightly clavate tip is often visible through the wall. The column is entirely bright red, a novel feature in this genus, and close inspection reveals a frilly margin around the anther and a minute red tooth that descends into the mouth of the spur. *Plants life size*

Aerangis luteo-alba (Kraenzlin) Schlechter var. *rhodosticta* (Kraenzlin) J. Stewart in *Kew Bulletin*, **34**(2): 310 (1979)
Angraecum luteo-album Kraenzlin in Engler, *Die Pflanzenwelt Ost-Afrikas*, C: 158 (1895)
Angraecum rhodostictum Kraenzlin in *Notizblatt des Botanischen Gartens und Museums zu Berlin*, **1**: 54 (1896)
Aerangis rhodosticta (Kraenzlin) Schlechter in *Beihefte zum Botanisches Centralblatt*, **36**(2): 113 (1918)

In 1895, the German botanist Fritz Kraenzlin described some small, yellowish-white flowered plants, collected in the eastern regions of Zaïre, as *Angraecum luteo-album*. Only a year later, in a quite different publication, he described other plants with very similar flowers from two collections as far apart as Cameroun and Ethiopia. But these had a bright red column that provided a unique contrast with the perianth and a feature of potential horticultural interest; he gave the name *Angraecum rhodostictum* to these specimens. In 1918 Rudolf Schlechter transferred both species to the genus *Aerangis*.

While a difference in colour of part of the flower is not by itself an acceptable criterion for species recognition, it can be used, if thought desirable to do so, at lower levels of classification. Thus two varieties of *Aerangis luteo-alba* are now recognised, with the colour of the column providing the difference between them, a difference that is presumably linked to a different pollinator and is therefore a biological as well as a morphological distinction. The white- or yellowish-columned variety, although recorded from several localities in eastern Zaïre and rumoured from western Uganda, is not currently available in cultivation. The red-columned variety, described by the appropriate and euphonious epithet *rhodosticta*, has now been collected from a wide belt across equatorial Africa, from Cameroun and the Central African Empire in the west, to Kenya and Ethiopia in the east. The first living plants that were exhibited in flower in England, in 1922, created a minor sensation and were given the provisional but, unfortunately, only temporary name, *Angraecum mirabile*.

This species is primarily an epiphyte of twigs and narrow branches, although it also occurs on tree trunks. It is often encountered near rivers and waterfalls, where the air is humid yet buoyant, and nearly always in very shady places. Strangely, it is one of those orchids that has adapted well to the man-made habitats provided by plantations and in some parts of Uganda was once declared a weed that was said to be endangering the coffee bushes on which it grew.

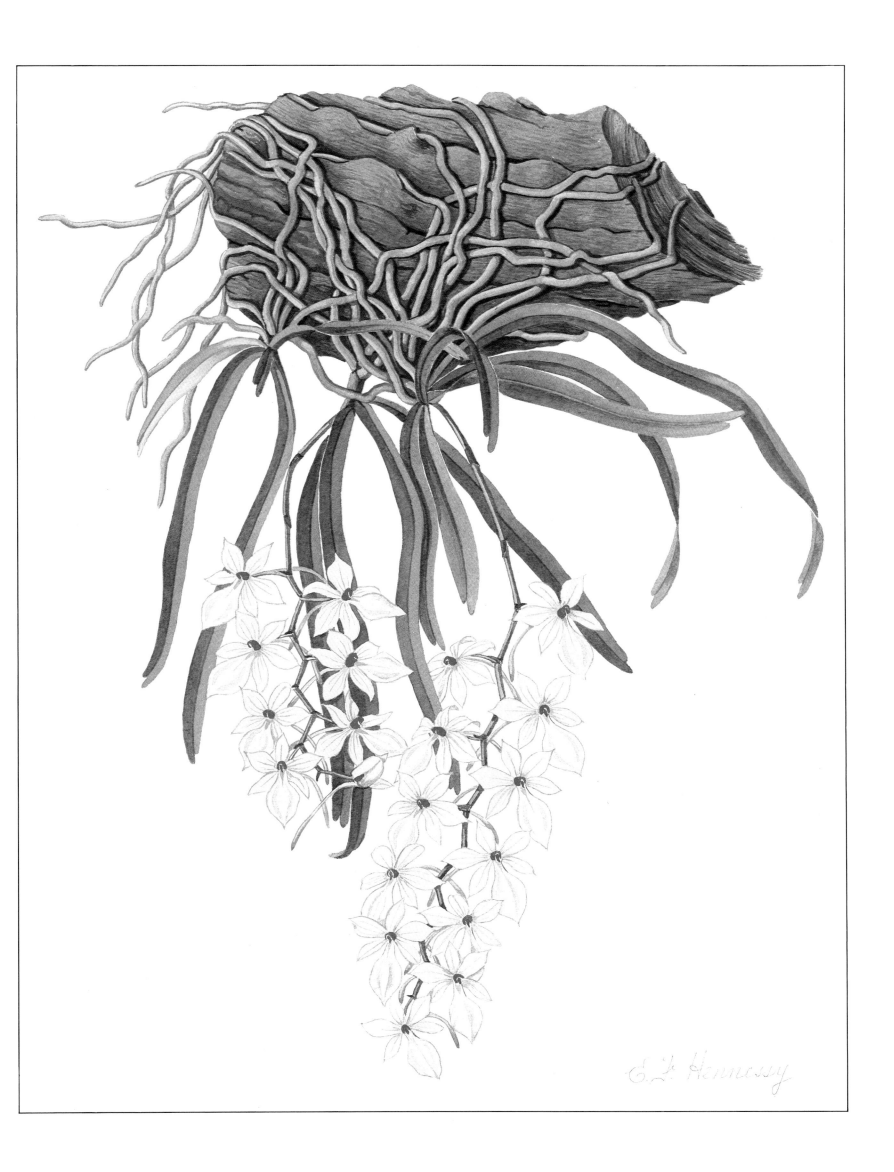

PLATE 32
Aerangis somalensis

A short-stemmed epiphyte with numerous very thick roots. Each plant bears two to six leaves that are remarkable for their leathery, sometimes almost succulent texture and for their greyish-green colour. The basic colour is enhanced by the raised, reticulate venation and is often imbued with a distinct reddish cast. The leaves are very variable in size, from 2–11 cm long and up to 3 cm wide. The inflorescences are usually pendent and arise below the leaves, each bearing four to seventeen flowers. The flowers are often tinged with pink, or there may be a greenish tone overlaying the basic white. The dorsal sepal is about 10 mm long and arches forward over the short, stout column. The lateral sepals and petals are spreading on either side of the column, and the former are often somewhat reflexed. The strap-shaped lip is often slightly twisted and bears a conspicuous nectary at its base in the form of a spur, 10–15 cm long, that is slightly inflated and darker coloured in its lower third. The stout column bears a narrow pointed rostellum, which projects forward across the entrance to the spur.   *Plant x4/5*

Aerangis somalensis (Schlechter) Schlechter in *Beihefte zum Botanisches Centralblatt*, **36**(2): 120 (1918)
Angraecum somalense Schlechter in Engler, *Botanische Jahrbucher*, **38**: 163 (1906)

Succulence is somewhat unexpected in an epiphytic orchid but the leaves of this species, while they feel tough and flabby like some of the modern substitutes for leather, resemble those of several succulent plants in substance and coloration. Most often the leaves are bluish- or greyish-green with a distinctly darker green venation. In some plants the leaves are entirely green, although more than one shade of green is present, but in many there is a strong development of reddish pigments that overlie the green colour throughout the life of the plant and fade less rapidly with age, so that old leaves become bright orange when the green pigments fade before they fall. The unusual colours, venation, and undulate margin of the leaves, all combine to create a striking plant, whose short stem is supported by a prolific development of thick greyish roots. The latter provide an abundant surface area for the absorption of the meagre amounts of moisture that are available in the habitats this species occupies. The plants appear to be well suited to the relict patches of forest and bush that line ephemeral streams in some of the semi-desert or steppe regions of eastern Africa. Valley bottoms and the base of isolated hills are places where cloud and mist accumulate with local and temporary changes in temperature, and these are the places to search for this unusual orchid.

The exact origin of this species is uncertain, since the Italian collectors who discovered it, Prince Eugenio Ruspoli and his companion, Domenico Riva, were wandering through the area along the border between Kenya, Somalia and Ethiopia, and did not record its precise location when they collected specimens in 1893. Its distribution in Ethiopia and eastern Kenya is now fairly well known, but there appear to be two huge gaps in its range, between south-eastern Kenya and southern Tanzania, and from the latter to the eastern part of the Transvaal in South Africa.

It has sometimes been confused with *Aerangis verdickii*, another species with a succulent habit and thick fleshy roots, but which has larger flowers with a longer spur and two raised, parallel crests along the base of the lip. Its leaves are different, too, although succulent, as they are usually much longer and thicker and lack the distinct pattern of venation that is characteristic of the leaves of *A. somalensis*.

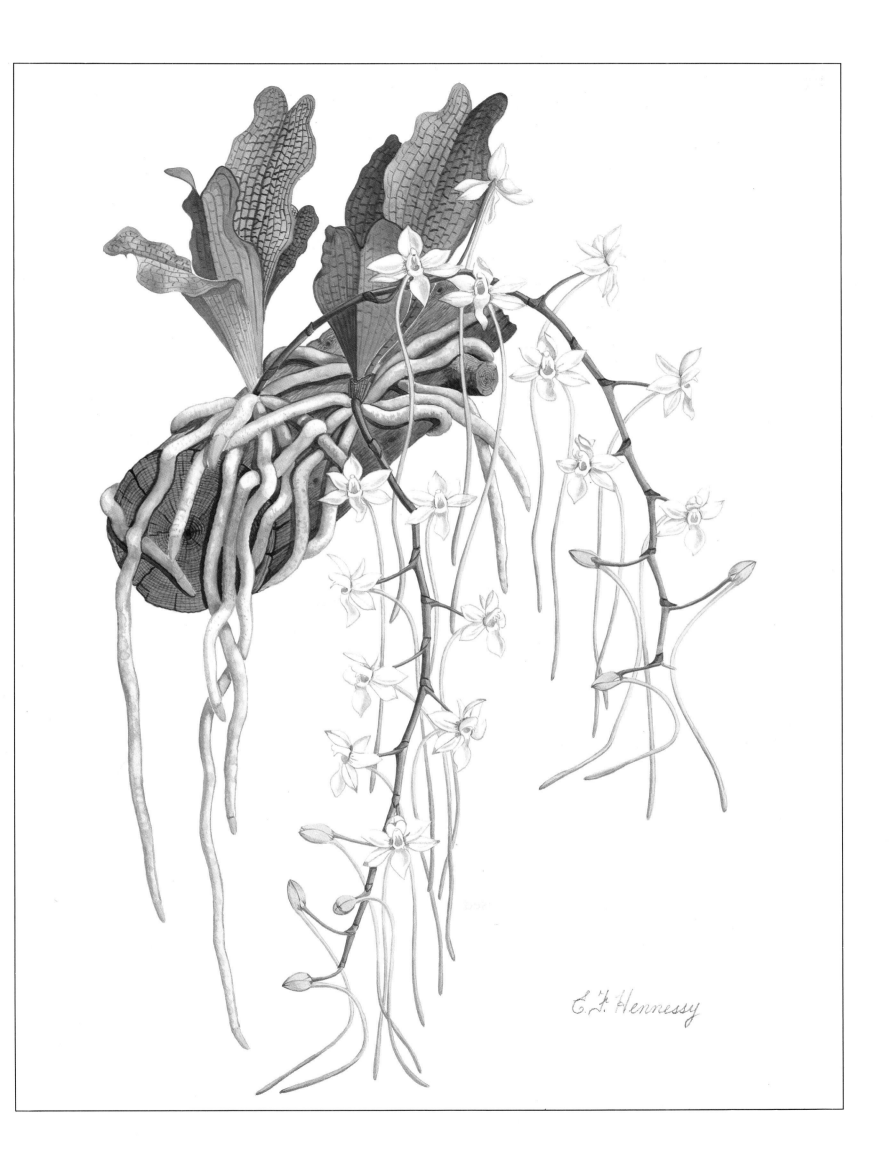

E. F. Hennessy

PLATE 33
Summerhayesia zambesiaca

A distinctive monopodial epiphyte, with leathery leaves and arching spikes of bold and striking flowers. In older plants only the apical part of the stem is leafy and the part below the leaves is covered by the remains of the sheathing leaf bases. The linear leaves are fleshy and carried in two neat rows that give the plant a fan-shaped appearance. Below the leaves the inflorescence is erect when it first begins to grow, but soon arches over and becomes pendent under the weight of the flowers that are regularly spaced along its upper half. The flowers are fleshy and almost waxy, greenish-yellow on the outer surface of all their parts and ivory white within. The concave lip is uppermost in the flower and bears a spur up to 20 cm long at its base. The lateral sepals are joined together behind the lip, and on their outer surface, as well as on that of the ovary and spur, there is a brownish, furry indumentum. *Plant x1/4; inflorescence x4/5*

Summerhayesia zambesiaca Cribb in *Kew Bulletin,* **32**: 185–7 (1977)

This striking species has been known in several parts of eastern central Africa for at least twenty years, but was recognised and formally named only very recently. The description of a new species of orchid is not a rare event and most of the delay in giving this plant a name arose from the fact that it did not quite fit into any of the recognised genera. When dealing with a large collection of orchids from Zambia and Zimbabwe, many of which proved to be new, the Kew orchidologist, Philip Cribb, found that this species most nearly resembled a West African orchid, then known as *Aerangis laurentii*. However, the present author had already discovered that the latter species differed in several distinct ways from all the known species of *Aerangis* and was considering a proposal to remove it to another genus, perhaps *Plectrelminthus*. The situation was resolved by Cribb's establishment of the new genus *Summerhayesia*, which now contains two species, *S. laurentii* and the one illustrated here. The generic name honours the late Victor S. Summerhayes (1892–1974), whose studies of African orchids have made a great contribution to our knowledge and understanding of them. In proposing this new genus, Cribb suggested that its closest affinities lie with both *Aerangis* and *Plectrelminthus*, but that it can be distinguished from both of them by its fleshy, ovate lip, by its slipper-shaped viscidium that fits over the tip of the rostellum, and by the tough, markedly folded leaves.

Plants of *Summerhayesia zambesiaca* are smaller than those of the West African species but the flowers are much larger with longer spurs. It grows both as an epiphyte and as a lithophyte in hot, humid areas of Zambia and on both sides of the border between Zimbabwe and Mozambique. Flowers are produced during the summer months, at various times between January and May, and last for three or four weeks on the plant. In the original description only five flowers are recorded on the inflorescence, but the plant illustrated here bore thirteen. It was kindly loaned for illustration by Ron and Terry Slater of Queensburgh in Natal, who collected it near Chipinga, in the Melsetter district of Zimbabwe, in 1973. A plant from western Mozambique that flowered in the author's greenhouse had nine flowers which all remained pale greenish-yellow in colour.

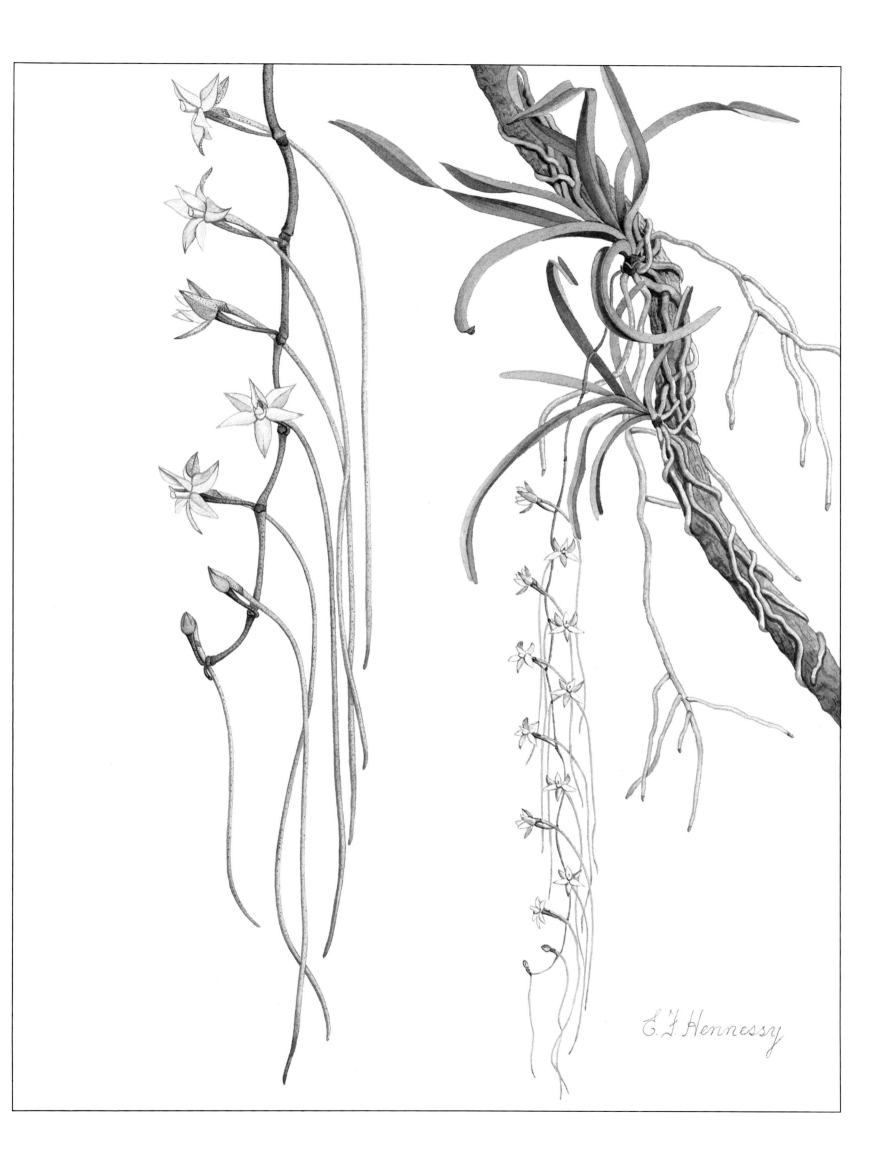

E. F. Hennessy

PLATE 34
Rangaeris muscicola

An erect epiphyte or lithophyte, with stout stems bearing thick greyish roots and closely overlapping leaves. The dull green leaves are V-shaped in cross section, and since they arise in two rows, very close together on the short stems, they give to each plant a neat, fan-shaped appearance. There are usually several inflorescences, arising in the axils of the lowermost leaves, each bearing two to eight flowers. From greenish buds, the flowers appear white when they first open but fade gradually to a creamy colour, and then turn pale apricot, becoming almost orange before they die. Each flower has a starry shape and is 2–3 cm in diameter. The broadly triangular lip bears a long sinuous spur that is 10–12 cm long.   *Plants life size*

Rangaeris muscicola (Reichenbach *filius*) Summerhayes in Hutchinson and Dalziel (eds.), *Flora of West Tropical Africa*, edition 1, **2**: 450 (1936)
Aeranthus muscicola Reichenbach *filius* in *Flora*, **48**: 190 (1865)

This ornamental species is one of the most widespread of African epiphytes. In the north of the continent, it has been recorded from Guinea and Sierra Leone in the west across to Kenya in the east, and in the south it extends as far as the Cape Province of South Africa. It is often an epiphyte on rain forest trees, but in Natal and other parts of South Africa it frequently grows as a lithophyte. The plants illustrated here were growing on and among huge blocks of Table Mountain sandstone at the lip of a deep gorge not very far from the sea. It has also been recorded as a lithophyte in Zambia and Malawi. But whether it is located on rocks or on trees, it is always found in localities where the environmental conditions are suitable for the growth of mosses, and a dense mat of these moisture-holding plants surrounds the roots and bases of the stems. Reichenbach must have been aware of this feature of its habitat when he named this species *muscicola*, which means 'associated with mosses'.

The stems of this species never become greatly elongated, but the plants increase in number and size by the development of axillary buds into shoots and eventually new stems. What appears to be a group of many plants growing closely together may in fact be clonal progeny from a single original plant. A cluster such as this provides several interlocking fans of stiff, folded leaves that often have a rather dull surface. The rigidity of their appearance becomes camouflaged when the inflorescences appear, bearing flowers that are at first pure white, and perfect, with the most delicious fragrance. Like those of several species of *Cyrtorchis*, however, they soon deepen in colour and are quite orange by the time they fold and fall.

Throughout its range this species produces its flowers during the rainy season, from December to February in South Africa, and through March and April further north. The flowers appear at their best and last longer while it is actually raining and atmospheric humidity is high. This observation provides a hint for growers of this delightful species, who are sometimes disappointed by its fugacious flowers. Given the correct environmental conditions, they last on the plant for two or three weeks, but if the atmosphere is too dry they fade much earlier.

PLATE 35
Mystacidium capense

A neat, dwarf epiphyte, with several pairs of leathery green leaves on its short erect stem, and numerous greyish roots at its base. The leaves are borne in two rows, and when old they disarticulate from the sheath along a pronounced abscission zone, so that the lower part of the stem is often covered with their sharp-edged remains. It is from the lower part of the stem that numerous arching or pendulous racemes of sweetly scented flowers arise regularly, every year. The flowers are white or cream with acuminate, recurved sepals and similar but slightly smaller petals. The lip resembles the petals but bears a pair of tooth-shaped lobes at the base, on either side of the column. The pale green spur is curved, approximately 5 cm long, and it is narrowly cylindrical in shape below the funnel-shaped entrance. *Plants life size*

Mystacidium capense (Linnaeus *filius*) Schlechter in *Beihefte zum Botanisches Centralblatt*, **36**(2): 125 (1918)
Epidendrum capense Linnaeus *filius*, *Supplementum Plantarum*, 407 (1781)
Limodorum longicorne Thunberg, *Prodromus plantarum capensium*, 3 (1794)
Angraecum capense (Linnaeus *filius*) Lindley, *The Genera and Species of Orchidaceous Plants*, 248 (1833)
Mystacidium filicorne Lindley in Hooker, *Companion to the Botanical Magazine*, **2**: 206 (1837)

Very few African orchids reached Europe as early as the eighteenth century and only a few were seen by Linnaeus himself. None are mentioned in the famous *Species Plantarum* of 1753, which is the starting-point for the modern nomenclature of plants. Linnaeus described eight species of Cape orchids in 1760, and a few more in three subsequent publications, but the collections made in the eastern Cape by Thunberg and Sparrman remained at Uppsala until the younger Linnaeus had succeeded his father as Professor of Botany there. In 1781 he described thirty-one species of South African orchids, including *Epidendrum capense*, the first of the epiphytic orchids from this continent to be sent to Europe. The description was based on the specimen collected by Thunberg, who redescribed it himself in 1794 as *Limodorum longicorne*.

When the English orchidologist, John Lindley, wrote his account of all the orchids then known in 1833, he proposed that Linnaeus's name should be transferred to the genus *Angraecum*. On examining other specimens, however, he realised that the column structure was quite different from that of any *Angraecum* he knew, although the habit of the plant was remarkably similar. From the front of the column, the three-lobed rostellum protrudes forward unprotected by the anther cap and bears two viscidia, each with a long slender stipe, between its papillose lateral lobes and smooth central lobe. So, in 1837, Lindley established the genus *Mystacidium*, deriving this name from the Greek word for moustache, presumably alluding to the papillose rostellum lobes of this species. He gave it the name of *M. filicorne*, although he was well aware that it had been described already under another name. Thus, these dainty and fragile-looking flowers have been known by several different epithets in the past, but are now widely recognised as *Mystacidium capense*.

Some of the first specimens seen in Europe came from the Fish River area of the eastern Cape Province. The species is still common in that region, and in parts of Natal and Swaziland where hot and humid summer weather alternates between heavy storms and dry intervals of several days' duration. In the winter months, temperatures are much lower, humidity almost disappears, and the dry periods are very prolonged. The orchid is always epiphytic and appears to grow equally successfully on the rough, often flaking bark of *Acacia* trees, and the smooth, even surface of succulent, giant species of *Euphorbia*.

E F Hennessy

PLATE 36
Mystacidium venosum

A tiny, dainty epiphyte with small leaves and numerous conspicuous roots. The roots are grey, and often spread radially from the base of the very short stem. Two to four oblong leaves with an unequally bilobed apex are normally present, but plants are sometimes leafless for prolonged periods. A number of arching racemes are often produced simultaneously and each bears five to eight small white flowers. The sepals and petals are narrow and acuminate, usually recurved at the tips. The lip is similar but has two rounded lobules at the base on either side of the entrance to the slender spur, which is 3–5 cm long. *Plants life size*

Mystacidium venosum Harvey ex Rolfe in Thiselton-Dyer (editor), *Flora Capensis*, **5**(3): 79 (1912)

This delightful miniature lays claim to fame by flowering during the period May to August when it is winter in the summer-rainfall areas of Southern Africa and very few orchids are in bloom. Flowers are produced with enthusiasm, usually on several pendent racemes that are massed to provide a perfect bouquet. Several plants growing close together provide a splendid sight by day, the surface cells of each flower sparkling in the sunlight, and a pervasive perfume adds to their attractiveness as darkness falls. In many ways the flowers are extremely similar to those of *M. capense*, on the previous plate, but they are always smaller in all respects and, of course, are produced very much earlier in the year. Dissection of the column reveals the much more slender rostellum, with positively bearded side lobes and a very narrow central lobe. The leaves are also very much smaller, and sometimes bear a quite distinct venation pattern, which presumably provided Harvey with the basis for the specific epithet, *venosum*.

The roots are the most conspicuous feature of the plants of this species. For much of the year they are its only visible feature, for the leaves may be shed during a dry winter or eaten away by slugs in a wet period of the summer. The extensive roots penetrate for long distances on the surface of the bark of the host tree, and through the upper layers of bark. Often they obtain shelter under the epiphytic lichens, which also enjoy the exposed positions in the habitat that the orchids favour. The roots turn greenish when it rains and reveal the fact that there are chloroplasts in the inner cortex to aid those in the leaves in the practice of photosynthesis. They are always apparent at the bright green root tip, which is not yet covered by the protective grey velamen. The surface of the roots is decorated with numerous striations, called pneumathodes, which are dark grey when the roots are dry but appear whitish when they become wet. These locally strengthened sites provide space for air exchange in wet conditions and extra support when dry.

Plants of this species are easily established and maintained in cultivation, on branches or pieces of bark. In the wild they are found in a variety of situations, in positions where they are fully exposed to the sun for at least part of the year, or in light or fairly heavy shade. They grow on a wide variety of trees, in the hot, humid habitats of the coastal forests, and in the cooler and misty heights of the temperate forests further inland.

PLATE 37
Cyrtorchis arcuata subspecies whytei

A large and handsome epiphytic plant, its upright stems covered with the sheathing remains of old leaf bases. The thick fleshy roots are borne on the older parts of the stems and also among the leaves. The leaves are carried in two rows and are produced alternately on either side of the stem. They are unequally bilobed at the apex and broad and leathery throughout their length. The inflorescences arise in the axils of the leaves and the flower-buds are hidden inside the broadly ovate bracts. The latter are pale green at first but turn dark brown or black by the time the flowers open. The flowers are white but turn yellow and then orange as they age. The long sepals, petals and lip are all recurved and very similar in size and shape. The stout curving spur is usually S-shaped, and the column is hidden inside the base of the perianth.   *Plant x4/5*

Cyrtorchis arcuata (Lindley) Schlechter ssp. *whytei* (Rolfe) Summerhayes in *Kew Bulletin*, **14**: 147 (1960)
Angraecum arcuatum Lindley in Hooker, *Companion to the Botanical Magazine*, **2**: 204 (1837)
Listrostachys whytei Rolfe in Thiselton-Dyer (editor), *Flora of Tropical Africa*, **7**: 155 (1897)

Cyrtorchis arcuata is an extremely widespread and variable species, ranging throughout the continent of Africa, south of the Sahara, from Ethiopia almost to the Cape and from Sierra Leone to Kenya. The late V.S. Summerhayes recognised four different subspecies, which can be differentiated by the size of their flowers and bracts, the length and shape of their leaves, and their geographical distribution.

The plant illustrated here was collected in Malawi, by Bob Campbell of Nairobi, and has been grown in cultivation since 1969. It represents the subspecies *whytei*, which has wider leaves and larger flowers with longer spurs than any of the other subspecies. It was named in honour of the first collector, the naturalist Alexander Whyte, whose specimen came from the plateau of Mount Mlanje in the early 1890s. The flowers are almost as large as those of *C. chailluana*, a West African species which is the largest in the genus, but they always have shorter spurs.

This subspecies occurs in two disjunct areas, one in Malawi and adjacent parts of Tanzania, and the other in the extreme west of Africa, in Sierra Leone, Liberia and Ghana. More recently it has been reported from northern Zambia, and there is a single gathering from north-eastern Tanzania that agrees well with the other material. Its habitat is usually the canopy of the relict forest trees that are found fringing rivers and streams, as well as that of broad-leaved woodland and the scattered trees of savanna vegetation. *Cyrtorchis chailluana* is a species of true rain forest vegetation, ranging throughout the Congo River basin and into adjacent areas. The present subspecies seems to replace it in slightly drier areas, while the subspecies *arcuata* from Southern Africa, and the widespread subspecies *variabilis* in tropical Africa, are found in a wide variety of habitats, but never in rain forest. The different forms of *C. arcuata* can be very similar, and trying to find names for them is sometimes a confusing and frustrating experience. It seems likely that the botanist is observing speciation in action among all these variable forms, which makes it very difficult to classify them into different categories at the moment. One is left with a choice: either every population represents a new species in the making, or there is one, single, widespread and variable species. Summerhayes preferred the latter view, but found it convenient to subdivide the species to a certain extent.

E. F. Hennessy

PLATE 38
Tridactyle gentilii

The finest species of this intriguing epiphytic genus. Old plants become long and pendent with many branching stems that become closely intertwined and form dense, tangled masses on the branches of trees. For much of their length the stems are bare or clothed only with the remains of sheathing leaf bases, and it is only towards the tip that a fan of short, fleshy leaves is borne. The inflorescences arise below the leaves and bear seven to twelve flowers very close together on a short zigzag rachis. The flowers are pale green, sweetly scented in the evening, and the central column and curiously constructed lip are their most conspicuous parts. The lip bears a thickened greenish spur, 5–8cm long, from a gaping cavity near its base. On either side of the spur entrance a pair of auricles extend outwards from the lip, which in its apical part is three-lobed. The middle lobe is short and acute, but the side lobes are much longer and fimbriate at their tips. The column often appears to be almost an upward extension of the lip. Near its apex it bears a very large stigmatic depression below the bright orange-brown anther cap that conceals the pollinia.   *Plants life size*

Tridactyle gentilii (De Wildeman) Schlechter in *Beihefte zum Botanisches Centralblatt*, **36**(2): 145 (1918)
Angraecum gentilii De Wildeman in *Notices sur les plantes utiles ou intéressantes de la flore du Congo*, **1**: 140 (1903)

Tridactyle is a genus of about thirty-six species of African epiphytes, a few of which also occur as lithophytes on sandstone or granite outcrops. In all the species the lip is more or less three-lobed, a feature which provided the basis for Schlechter's generic name. In several species, including *T. gentilii*, the side lobes of the lip are further divided so that they appear finely fringed. At the base of the lip, on either side of the entrance to the spur, there are additional outgrowths, termed auricles, which vary in shape and size but are quite conspicuous in this species. Only a few of the species bear white flowers; mostly they are pale yellow or brownish and sometimes green. In some species the inflorescences bear a number of flowers, although they are rarely longer than the leaves, while in others only small groups of a few flowers are almost sessile on the woody stem.

We have chosen the largest-flowered species of *Tridactyle* for illustration on the accompanying plate. It is also of interest on account of its distribution. The species was described originally from Zaïre and by 1968 it was also known from Ghana, northern Nigeria, east Cameroun and Zambia. Since then it has been discovered in western Uganda and, very recently, in northern Natal, South Africa. The plant illustrated was collected there in 1979 by Kevin Rogers and Michael O'Connor, who kindly loaned it for the purpose. It is sometimes described as a rain forest species but, if so, it is also able to survive in areas from which rain forest has now receded. In Natal it has been found in a very narrow strip of forest, fringing a river, and in Nigeria it is currently recorded only from the wooded Plateau Province where true rain forest is no longer found. A glance at a vegetation map of Africa reveals that this species is perhaps more correctly described as a denizen of moist woodland and savanna regions. It may yet be found in some of the intervening countries with similar climates and vegetation, such as Zimbabwe, Mozambique and Angola.

The growth habit of this species, and of others in this genus, is typically vandaceous. The stems branch frequently and new shoots arise from dormant axillary buds when the apical meristem is damaged or dies. Large clumps of plants are easily established and grow well in cultivation under the same conditions as the flat-leaved species of *Vanda*. Plenty of warmth and sunlight, combined with high humidity by day and a fall in temperature at night, are the chief requirements for successful cultivation.

E F Hennessy

PLATE 39
Polystachya affinis

An evergreen epiphyte with a flattened, creeping growth habit. The pseudobulbs are round, flat and more or less orbicular, crowded together on the inconspicuous woody rhizome. From the apex of each one a pair of dark green, glossy leaves or sometimes a solitary leaf arises, and the many-flowered branching inflorescence is borne in its axil, ensheathed in several membranous bracts. The inflorescence axis and the outer surface of both the bracts and the golden-brownish flowers, are all softly hairy, almost downy to the touch. Because the inflorescence arches over, the dorsal sepal is uppermost in the flowers. The broader lateral sepals are united at the base and decurrent along the extended base of the column, to which the three-lobed lip is also attached. The broad lip is strongly recurved, softly hairy along the central, basal part of the middle lobe, and streaked with vertical red lines on its erect side lobes. *Plant life size*

Polystachya affinis Lindley in *The Genera and Species of Orchidaceous Plants*, 73 (1830)

This was the second species of *Polystachya* to be illustrated and described in *Curtis's Botanical Magazine*, in 1845, having been grown at Kew since its introduction there from Sierra Leone. The first species, too, figured in 1839 and now known as *P. galeata*, also came from this part of West Africa. Both species are now known from a wide belt across the equatorial and tropical regions of the continent. They are recorded from most of the countries of West Africa and as far south and east as Gabon and Zaïre, in the case of *P. galeata*, whereas *P. affinis* grows in these countries as well, and extends eastward as far as Uganda.

The plant illustrated was collected in Liberia in 1968, by Alex Forbes-Watson, and flowers regularly in a very warm and humid greenhouse. Pot culture suits it well, though in the wild it is reported from the vertical trunks of trees, well below the forest canopy, and usually on rather bare trunks where it is exposed to the dancing rays of the full sun as they penetrate the moving forest canopy, for at least part of the day.

Polystachya is a large genus of at least two hundred species. While it is one of only two epiphytic orchid genera with a worldwide distribution (the other is *Bulbophyllum*), the majority of species are restricted to Africa and most of them are found in the tropical and subtropical forests. The genus is readily divisible into a number of easily recognisable sections, and the species illustrated here gives its name to the section *Affines*. Like the other species in this section, it has rather compressed pseudobulbs that are somewhat flattened against the substratum; each one is surmounted by a slender stem bearing two or three leaves and a terminal inflorescence. Most of the species in the section have hairy stems, bracts and flowers.

Although it is normally described as an epiphytic genus, several African species of *Polystachya* are usually found on rocks. In Zambia, two species in this section, *P. zambesiaca* and *P. villosa*, are recorded on granite slabs and in the pockets of soil and leaf litter that accumulate between them, as well as on trees. Perhaps this catholicity of habit in the wild accounts for the ease with which all these species may be grown in cultivation.

E.F.Hennessy

PLATE 40
Polystachya bella

A lovely epiphyte that grows in dense tufts. The pseudobulbs, which are oval and compressed so that they are two-edged, stand very close together, each somewhat above the last, on the short basal rhizome. Each new growth bears one or two strap-shaped leaves and an apical inflorescence. The pseudobulb develops, with its attendant roots, after flowering. The inflorescence is softly hairy and is conspicuous at first for its long, pointed bracts and buds, and later for the size and clarity of its golden flowers. The flowers are not resupinate and are 1.5–2 cm long. The lateral sepals are united to form a conspicuous mentum at the top of each flower. The intermediate sepal and petals are narrow and pointed. The lip is three-lobed: the side lobes stand erect on either side of the column while the narrow middle lobe is sharply reflexed. Along its centre line it bears a bright orange streak, which is usually just visible at the point where the lip emerges between the lateral sepals.

Plant x4/5

Polystachya bella Summerhayes in *Kew Bulletin,* **14**: 137 (1960)

Although it was not formally named and described until 1960, this species has been known in cultivation for more than fifty years. Originally introduced to Europe from Kenya, it is now known also from Uganda, although rarely collected there. Recently a cream-coloured form was discovered in the Kalinzu Forest of western Uganda, by Herman and Ria Meyer, and it proves to be just as easy to grow. Possibly its flowers are slightly larger than the golden ones of the better-known plants; they are certainly remarkably fine, and the bright orange flash on the lip provides just as striking a contrast to the velvety texture of the rest of the flower as it does in the form illustrated here.

This plant was collected from a fallen tree in the forests near Kericho, a part of Kenya that is famous for its tea plantations. In many parts of the world, where the climate and soil conditions are suitable for the cultivation of tea, orchids are a conspicuous feature of the native flora. There are still several parts of Africa, in Kenya and Uganda, the highlands of southern Tanzania, Malawi, eastern Zimbabwe and the eastern Transvaal, as well as the rolling lowlands of Transkei, where the relict forest patches that have not been removed or replaced by tea support a most interesting and varied epiphyte flora. This includes many orchids, and a large number of species of *Polystachya*, sometimes several in the same tree.

In cultivation the substratum, in the pot in which the plant is grown or the branch on which it is mounted, appears to be less important than correct atmospheric conditions for the healthy growth of this species. Pseudobulbs develop from the basal rhizome, each one slightly above the other, for several years before any roots are produced. Thus moisture and its dissolved chemicals must be absorbed through the leaves. A buoyant yet very humid atmosphere is essential, but, judging by the wide altitudinal range over which this species is found in the Kericho district of Kenya, temperature is much less important. Misty nights and mornings, combined with warm sunny days, are not easy to arrange in a greenhouse, but in addition to a drop in temperature at night, a change in humidity during the day, coupled with plenty of air movement, is very beneficial to the growth of this species. In a well-tended plant, the basal rhizome branches frequently, so that a specimen of very pleasing size can be obtained from a small division within a few years.

E. F. Hennessy

PLATE 41
Polystachya ottoniana

A miniature, tufted species with conical pseudobulbs that form large clusters from the frequently branching rhizome. The pseudobulbs are enclosed in membranous sheaths when young but become bare, wrinkled and leafless as they age. Two or three linear or linear-lanceolate leaves are borne at the apex of the developing pseudobulb and the infloresence appears at the tip of this new growth between the last-formed pair of leaves. A crop of one to six showy flowers is produced from each new stem every spring. They are basically white in colour but charmingly tinted with pink or mauve, and a deep yellow stripe embellishes the midline of the three-lobed lip. The violet anther cap occupies a prominent position at the end of the column and is easily detached while still enclosing four ovoid pollinia, a pair in each of its two cells.   *Plant life size; flower and half flower x4; anther cap and pollinia x12; column and anther x10*

Polystachya ottoniana Reichenbach *filius* in *Hamburg Gartenzeitung,* **11**: 249 (1855)

This species grows as an epiphyte or lithophyte in well-lit situations in forests, on trees and rocks, on the rocky banks of streams, and on rock outcrops in mountainous areas. It enjoys very cool conditions during the resting period and is found growing only in places where the environment is inimical to growth for several months of the year, so that a complete rest is assured. During this period the leaves are often shed and plants are visible only as a mass of squat, wrinkled pseudobulbs which form a rough cushion on the host branch or boulder. Under good growing conditions and in cultivation, the leaves may be retained for several years. Like *P. pubescens*, illustrated on Plate 43, this species is found in the forested parts of South Africa, Transkei and Swaziland. But it is tolerant, too, of very much cooler conditions than that species enjoys, and is found at much higher altitudes, even in places where frost and snow are not uncommon during the winter.

This is one of the many species of African orchids that were described by H.G. Reichenbach. He named it in honour of C. Friedrich Otto, who had been curator of the Berlin Botanic Garden for many years. In fact a poor specimen had been sent to Europe many years earlier, in the collections of J.F. Drège, but it was not in the flowering stage, and Lindley, who described it briefly with many other specimens of orchids collected by Drège, was unable to determine what genus it represented. Subsequently, many of the early botanical collectors of eastern South Africa, including Miss Pegler, Mrs Hutton, Mrs Barber in the eastern Cape, and Mrs Saunders in Natal, added pressed plants of this species to the collections they sent to the herbarium of the Royal Botanic Gardens, Kew.

The plant chosen for this illustration is known locally as the white form of the species and was loaned by Ron and Terry Slater of Queensburgh in Natal. The specimens that Reichenbach described when he named this species bore rather large white flowers with a deep yellow line on the mid-lobe of the lip. Today, two differently coloured forms are attributed to this species in South Africa. It is not certain, however, that the plants with yellowish-green flowers, which are usually produced rather earlier in the season and are slightly smaller than the white ones, are a form of this species: they may be representatives of another species that is more widespread in Africa, or they may prove to be undescribed. Careful, comparative studies of all the available material that is referable to the section *Humiles*, of which *P. ottoniana* is the type, may reveal that there are additional specimens still awaiting formal diagnosis, description and naming. Like *P. ottoniana*, all the species in this section are characterised by small or minute plants that bear relatively large flowers.

PLATE 42
Polystachya porphyrochila

A moisture-loving epiphyte, with pseudobulbs standing in neat rows on mossy branches of rain-forest trees. The pseudobulbs are narrowly ovoid or conical but slightly compressed so that they are nearly two-edged. Each bears a single leaf, hard and tough in texture, and articulated with the pseudobulb 2 cm or more above the apex. The inflorescence is shorter than the leaf, flattened and two-edged, gradually becoming wider towards the flowers. Several flowers are borne, successively, from the four-sided rachis, each one supported by a boat-shaped, acuminate bract. The flowers are creamy-white or ivory-coloured, with the lip partly dark red-purple. The column also shows this colour on the anther cap, which is basically purple but crowned with a round white crest. All the parts are thick and waxy and each flower lasts a long time on the plant.

Plant x4/5

Polystachya porphyrochila J. Stewart in *American Orchid Society Bulletin,* **42**: 590–593 (1973)

This fine species bears the largest flowers so far described in the genus. Unfortunately it could not be named *grandiflora*, or *macrantha*, since these epithets had already been used once for another species of *Polystachya*, now known as *P. galeata*. The adjective *porphyrochila* was coined in allusion to the red-purple border of the lip which, in its way, is as striking as the size of the flower.

As yet this species is known only from the Uluguru Mountains in Tanzania, but it has been collected there more than once. The habitat is a beautiful montane rain-forest, where a wealth of mosses and ferns grows epiphytically on the branch of every tree. It was first collected in April 1970, by a Hungarian botanist, Thomas Pocs, who was interested in all the epiphytes, but primarily in the moss flora of the area. The recognition and description of this striking species is thus somewhat reminiscent of the introduction to Europe of the genus *Cattleya* from South America. In 1818, some pseudobulbs of *C. labiata* were sent from Rio de Janeiro as packing material around other tropical plants including mosses and ferns. They were grown to the flowering stage by William Cattley, who was curious to see what kind of plant they might turn out to be. In the case of this *Polystachya*, however, the pseudobulbs were sent alone to the author, wrapped in newspaper, the mosses and ferns being preserved for other investigations by Pocs. The developing inflorescence the specimen bore was at once intriguing. It looked very different from any of the species of *Polystachya* already known from that area, and from any of the known species in the section *Cultriformes*, which is characterised by a single leaf at the apex of each pseudobulb. The waiting period while the buds developed was one of eager anticipation, a period that ended in excitement and delight as the first bud enlarged, swelled, cracked, opened and revealed the surprising bloom.

This flower illustrates rather clearly several of the generic characters of *Polystachya*. The ovary is not twisted, so that the intermediate sepal is borne on the lower side of the flower. It is opposite the lip, which is attached, at its base, to the upward-projecting foot of the column. The lip emerges from the prominent mentum, which is almost a double chin in this case, formed where the lateral sepals are also attached to the foot of the column.

In cultivation *P. porphyrochila* has proved remarkably easy, growing alongside the plant of *P. affinis* in Plate 39, but bearing flowers for a greater proportion of the year. Each bloom opens in succession and seven or eight are borne on an inflorescence, each lasting more than a month. Fortunately, the flowers can be self-pollinated, and fertile seed was obtained, sown, and germinated on one occasion. By ill luck, the seedlings died when the flask became contaminated with bacteria, but further attempts will be made to raise and disseminate plants of this very attractive species.

E. F. Hennessy

PLATE 43
Polystachya pubescens

A pretty epiphyte or lithophyte of compact and tidy habit. The conical, elongated, or spindle-shaped pseudobulbs are encased in membranous sheaths when young, which soon become brownish and transparent and eventually disintegrate. Two or three lanceolate or elliptic leaves are borne at the apex of each pseudobulb and while all these vegetative parts are still developing the flowering stem surmounts them. The inflorescences are softly hairy and bear many flowers, up to thirty in a well-grown specimen though seldom as many in the wild. The golden-orange flowers are not resupinate, so that the lip is held in the uppermost position and the dorsal sepal points downward. The lateral sepals are broad, concave, and conspicuously streaked with dark red horizontal lines that run longitudinally along the topmost side of each. The ovate petals are as broad as the dorsal sepal and a clear golden-yellow. The three-lobed lip is comparatively small, veined with red, and bears a mass of white silky hairs on each of its side lobes. The short column is greatly extended laterally, just below the golden anther cap, to form a wide, red-coloured border around the deep and glistening stigmatic cavity. *Plant life size*

Polystachya pubescens (Lindley) Reichenbach *filius* in Walpers, *Annales botanices systematicae*, **6**: 643 (1863)
Epiphora pubescens Lindley in Hooker, *Companion to the Botanical Magazine*, **2**: 201 (1837)

This species was described as the 'hairy-stemmed *Polystachya*' when it was illustrated in *Curtis's Botanical Magazine* in 1866 but later authors have assumed that the name *pubescens* was chosen in allusion to the white hairs on the side lobes of the lip. The species was first described as early as 1837, and only the ovaries are mentioned as being hairy in the original description. The specimens that he saw puzzled the English botanist, John Lindley, and he established a new genus, *Epiphora*, for them, coining a name that referred to the epiphytic habit. He noted, however, that the specimens somewhat resembled species of *Polystachya*, although he drew attention to the rather wide open flowers, the protracted base of the column and the shape of the lip.

Although frequently occurring as an epiphyte, this species also grows very often on rocks. Some of the most highly coloured forms, and those with a good deal of reddish pigment in the leaves, are found in the shallow pockets of soil that accumulate among rock outcrops, often where they receive the glare of full sunlight for much of the day. Throughout its range this species is subjected to a prolonged dry season during the cooler, winter months. A distinct rest is assured and new growth begins as soon as the days begin to lengthen in the spring. Flowers are produced on the new growths between September and December and new roots arise at the base of these new stems a little later, when plenty of moisture is available from early rains.

The plant specimens described by Lindley were collected by the German explorer and traveller, J.F. Drège. He spent eight years travelling in the Cape and Natal provinces collecting many thousands of pressed plants and other natural history specimens for sale. The specimens Lindley saw came from the area near Port Elizabeth, in the eastern part of Cape Province, but were not the first to be collected: the English explorer, William Burchell, had found the same species near Grahamstown a few years earlier.

Today this species is known throughout the summer-rainfall area of South Africa. It occurs near the sea and in many localities inland that are frost-free. It is well-known in the eastern Cape Province, Transkei and Natal, and has been recorded also from Swaziland and the eastern Transvaal.

PLATE 44
Eulophia clavicornis

An early-flowering terrestrial plant, whose flowering stems emerge as the first sign of active growth in spring. They, and their accompanying leafy shoot, grow out from the tip of a subterranean, moniliform rhizome. The leaves are always less than half the length of the inflorescence at flowering time, but later reach a length of 30 cm and are slightly fleshy in texture. The scape is thick, rather succulent and reddish-purple in colour; it may reach a height of 45 cm, but is usually much smaller, and it bears several clasping sheaths in the region below the flowers. Six or eight flowers are borne as a rule but the number varies from three to eighteen. Each part of the perianth is approximately 2 cm long but rather variable in colour. The sepals are purplish-green to dark reddish-purple, while the petals are white or pale purplish-pink tinged with darker purple or violet. The lip bears an elongated spur at its base and on its front surface a series of parallel crests, which form low ridges in the basal part and rise to form dentate or papillose lamellae towards the lip apex. These crests may be pale pink in colour, or straw yellow, sometimes tipped with purple or violet, while the parallel veins on either side of the crests are always dark purple. The flowers are short-lived and the greenish-purple capsules develop quickly from the ribbed, inferior ovary, each one bearing the remains of the dried flower at its tip.

Plants x4/5 and x2/5

Eulophia clavicornis Lindley in Hooker, *Companion to the Botanical Magazine*, **2**: 202 (1837)

The generic name *Eulophia* refers to the 'plume', or crests, on the lip, which all the species exhibit in some degree. The flowers are very variable in size, from less than 1 cm to 5–6 cm in length or diameter, and the crests may appear in the form of broad or narrow ridges, or lamellae, short or long hairs, or papillae, a combination of lamellae and papillae, or may be reduced to only two tooth-like projections near the lip base.

More than two hundred species of *Eulophia* are distributed throughout the warmer regions of the world, including America, Australia and India, but by far the larger proportion is in Africa. Over seventy-five species were recorded recently in Zambia and nearly forty are known in South Africa. They grow in a wide variety of habitats, from swamps to sand dunes, from seasonally dry grasslands to arid woodlands and wet rain forests, and may have their conspicuous pseudobulbs above ground level or hidden well below the surface.

In many species the flowers appear before the leaves and plants must be visited more than once, or grown in cultivation, before all the details of their structure can be recorded fully. *Eulophia clavicornis* grows from an underground rhizome in which each annual growth, or pseudobulb, has an irregular shape and is curiously flattened like a hand of ginger. The pseudobulbs appear strung together, like a chain of roughly formed, giant beads. They often branch and it is not unusual to find, on excavation, that several flowering stems of different ages, like the group depicted here, are all part of the same plant.

This species is known only from South Africa and the neighbouring countries of Transkei, Lesotho and Swaziland. It is a grassland plant and is conspicuous in early spring, or when the surrounding vegetation has been removed by burning. The flowering racemes emerge from the bare soil rapidly and the pale, nodding flowers soon attract an insect pollinator. It is rare to find plants in the field with their pollinia still intact, and a pendulous fruit develops from nearly every flower.

E. F. Hennessy

PLATE 45
Eulophia odontoglossa

A widespread terrestrial species with an elegant, slender habit. The flowers and leaves arise from separate shoots at the growing tip of the subterranean rhizome. The vegetative shoot bears one to three leaves that are almost or fully developed at flowering time, up to 100 cm long and 1–2 cm wide. The tall flowering-spike is completely encased in closely overlapping sheaths, which turn brown or straw-coloured while the spike is still young. There are seven to thirty dainty, golden-yellow flowers, each supported by a papery bract. The sepals and petals are each about 1 cm long and a little paler in colour than the three-lobed lip. The latter has a minute, almost vestigial spur at its base and a large middle lobe with a finely toothed margin. Behind the broad and rounded apex the lip is decorated by numerous slender papillae, which are reddish-brown at the base, and in the basal half it bears a pair of elevated yellow ridges in front of the brownish-red lining of the mentum or spur. The arching column is also brownish-red near its base and golden-yellow at the apex.

Plants life size

Eulophia odontoglossa Reichenbach *filius* in *Linnaea*, **19**: 373 (1846)

The leaves of *Eulophia* species vary in length and shape, but they are basically of two distinct kinds: either fleshy and conduplicate as in *E. clavicornis* (Plate 44) and *E. speciosa* (Plate 46) or plicate as in *E. streptopetala* (Plate 47) and in the species illustrated here. The plicate leaves are usually larger and very much thinner than the conduplicate ones. Usually, they are present at the time the plants flower, and often they are already fully developed at this stage.

This charming species is remarkable for its wide distribution throughout the African continent. In the tropical regions it is known from Guinea and Sierra Leone across to Kenya in the east and south to Zambia, Zimbabwe and Angola. It is also found in Southern Africa, in the warmer, lower altitudes in the eastern part of Cape Province and Natal and at somewhat higher elevations in Swaziland and Transvaal. It grows in various kinds of lateritic soil and has been collected both on well-drained slopes and in marshy places.

Throughout its range the species is always recognisable by the closely overlapping, straw-coloured sheaths that encase the flowering stem. But its flowers are extremely variable, particularly in their colour range. The golden-yellow form is one of the prettiest and is the commonest in South Africa, but in tropical Africa there are many variants. The flowers can be white, yellow or greenish with brown or purple markings, or sometimes completely brownish or purplish. Despite this variation, they are always characterised by the short, almost vestigial spur at the base of the lip, and the densely papillose midlobe with its finely toothed margin.

Perhaps because of this variation, the species has been described many times in different parts of the continent. In addition to the epithet *odontoglossa*, which refers to the teeth-like projections on the surface of the lip, it has received sixteen other names at various times, based on specimens from different parts of the continent. Some of these epithets reflect the place of origin, such as *shupangae*, *panganiana* and *durbanensis*, and a few were given in honour of the collector, including *johnstonii* and *holstiana*, but most refer to the colour of the flowers. Such epithets as *chrysantha* and *aurea* clearly indicate that the specimens bore golden blooms, while *ochracea* and *brunneo-rubra* suggest much duller flowers. For a long time, in South Africa, this species was known as *E. papillosa*, a name that also refers to the projections on the lip. Recently, however, research has revealed that the name *E. odontoglossa*, which was published nearly fifty years earlier, was used for identical specimens, also collected in Natal, so the species must be known henceforth by this no less attractive name.

PLATE 46
Eulophia speciosa

An ornamental terrestrial orchid with robust spikes of showy blossoms. The moniliform pseudobulbs are usually underground and the youngest one bears several thick almost succulent leaves, which reach a length of 60 cm before the flowering scapes emerge from a separate shoot. The inflorescence is usually 40–60 cm tall, but may reach 120 cm or more in shaded conditions in the wild and in cultivated plants. The sheaths are short, so that part of the bare green scape is exposed between successive nodes. Ten to thirty flowers are borne, successively, each one supported by a fairly conspicuous bract. The small, pale green sepals are reflexed towards the ovary. The large, round or ovate yellow petals are spreading and the three-lobed lip appears to project forward between them. At its base the lip bears a short blunt spur and the side lobes are united to the base of the column. The central part of the lip is convex in shape with the sides of the midlobe deflexed, while the apex is somewhat incurved. The lip is yellow, a rather deeper yellow along the crested, convex centre, and there are a few purple lines radiating from the throat on to the side lobes.   *Plant life size*

Eulophia speciosa (R. Brown ex Lindley) Bolus in *Journal of the Linnean Society*, **25**: 184 (1889)
Lissochilus speciosus R. Brown ex Lindley, *Collectanea Botanica*, t. 31 (1821) and Lindley in *Edwards's Botanical Register*, **7**: t. 573 (1821)

This is one of many South African flowering plants that was first introduced to Europe as a living specimen. The underground rhizome was sent from Cape Town to England and the plant flowered there first in 1821. Robert Brown described it as a species of his new genus *Lissochilus*, and the description and a detailed coloured plate were published by Lindley. The generic name, *Lissochilus*, was published, quite correctly, two years earlier than the name *Eulophia*. Brown, and several other botanists, thought that the two genera could be distinguished, the former having small, reflexed sepals and larger petals, whereas in the latter the sepals and petals were said to be similar in shape and size. But the two genera were merged at the end of the last century and the name *Eulophia* became widely used for all the species. By international agreement this has been accepted as the valid name so that the earliest name, *Lissochilus speciosus*, has become a synonym, and this species is well known in South Africa as *Eulophia speciosa*. In other parts of eastern Africa, from Zimbabwe north to Kenya, it is known by several other names, but it is anticipated that the latter, correct name for this very striking species will soon be widely accepted.

In many parts of its range, *E. speciosa* is found in very sandy soil and even on sand dunes at the edge of the beach. Elsewhere it is found in lateritic, reddish soils and in black clay. All these soils dry out for a considerable period each year and in cultivation a dry period, when water is completely withheld from the pot, is essential once flowering has been completed.

The flowering period of this species is very prolonged. In the wild and in cultivation the handsome spikes remain impressive for at least two months, although the lowermost flowers fall after two or three weeks. The plant used for this illustration has grown in the artist's garden in Durban, for many years, without any special attention.

E.F. Hennessy

PLATE 47
Eulophia streptopetala

A robust terrestrial plant, with conspicuous conical pseudobulbs situated at ground level or protruding slightly above it. The leaves of each new growth develop before the pseudobulb, and later in the season each one is shed from a distinct abscission layer near its base, leaving part of its petiole atop the remaining pseudobulb. The leaves are thin, somewhat pleated, with several conspicuous veins on the lower surface, and often of enormous size, reaching 75 cm in length and 11 cm in width at maturity. The inflorescences arise from the base of the previous year's growth and in robust specimens reach 2.5 m in height. They may be simple or sparingly branched and bear thirty to fifty flowers over a prolonged period. The scape is slender for its height, and bears a few tightly clasping sheaths. There is a striking contrast of coloration in the flowers. The sepals are basically green, but variously mottled with purplish-brown. They make a triangular frame for the bright yellow petals, which are often twisted forward so that the paler yellow, inner surface is hidden from view. The middle lobe of the lip is also yellow with brighter yellow crests, while the pale yellow side lobes at its base are striped with dull purple.

Plant x1/5; inflorescence life size

Eulophia streptopetala Lindley in *Edwards's Botanical Register*, **12**: t. 1002 (1826)
Lissochilus krebsii Reichenbach *filius* in *Linnaea*, **20**: 685 (1847)
Eulophia krebsii (Reichenbach *filius*) Bolus in *Journal of the Linnean Society*, **25**: 185 (1889)

This handsome species is widely distributed in eastern Africa, from Eritrea in the north to the eastern Cape Province of South Africa. Like many other African orchids, it has been the recipient of several different names in different parts of its range, and it was widely known as *Eulophia krebsii* for many years. But Lindley described it as *E. streptopetala* more than twenty years before Reichenbach named it *Lissochilus krebsii* and the former name has now become widely accepted.

Lindley had the habit, which many people would applaud, of coining English names for the orchids he described, as well as Latin ones. He called this species the 'twisted-petaled *Eulophia*', and the twisted claw of the broad petals of this species is, indeed, one of its most distinctive features. Unless one looks up into the face of the flower, it is often difficult to see more than the darker outer surface of the petals, since the twist ensures that they fall forward slightly on either side of the column.

This is one of the easiest species of *Eulophia* to maintain in cultivation. Its conical pseudobulbs somewhat resemble those of the well-known genus *Cymbidium* and they grow just as easily in a loose, well-drained mixture. Once their growth is completed and the leaves begin to absciss, a dry period of rest is indicated, similar to that which the species would be subjected to throughout most of its natural range, where rainfall is heaviest in the warmer, growing months and may be completely absent when conditions are cooler.

In the wild, this species has an interesting idiosyncrasy, since it is found always among shrubs, trees or large herbs and often among rocks where it receives some shelter and there is good drainage around its roots. It is never encountered in open grassland, or in forest, except along the margins, but has adapted well to *Eucalyptus* plantations in Natal and the Transvaal. The flowering-spike is produced during the summer months and is often long and spindly, requiring some support from the surrounding vegetation. It is usually simple at first but after the earliest flowers have fallen, one or more subsidiary spikes may emerge from a node lower down on the peduncle.

E.F. Hennessy

PLATE 48
Oeceoclades lonchophylla

A dainty shade-loving terrestrial species with unusual leaves and pale but delightful flowers. The plants bear more or less aerial pseudobulbs and few rather thick and whitish roots. Each dark green pseudobulb is surmounted by a single leaf that has a broad, oblong, glossy green lamina at the end of its long, slender, somewhat grooved petiole. One or two branching inflorescences are produced from the base of the newest pseudobulb. They may bear fifty flowers or more but there are usually not more than twenty open at any time and plants are often less prolific. The narrow sepals are yellowish-green, tinged with purple at the tips, and the petals are similarly coloured though often more distinctly spotted with purple. They are shorter and broader than the sepals and stand upright in a matching pair behind the column. The lip is the largest part of the perianth: it is conspicuously four-lobed; the basal side lobes are striped with purple while the two front lobes are greenish-cream; between the side lobes, towards the base, a two-ridged yellowish callus is evident immediately below the greenish-purple column.

Plant x3/4

Oeceoclades lonchophylla (Reichenbach *filius*) Garay and Taylor in *Botanical Museum Leaflets, Harvard University,* **24**: 264–5 (1976)
Eulophia lonchophylla Reichenbach *filius* in *Flora,* **68**: 542 (1885)
Eulophia dissimilis Dyer in *Flowering Plants of Africa,* **27**: t. 1066 (1949)

It happens not infrequently in modern botany that careful study of the work of much earlier botanists reveals mistakes made by their successors in interpreting their work or even in ignoring it completely. Thus the name *Oeceoclades*, introduced by Lindley in 1832, and formally published by him in 1859, was ignored by the German botanist Pfitzer in 1887 when he proposed the generic name *Eulophidium* for one of the same plants. Since that time several striking terrestrial orchids, which differ from the well-known genus *Eulophia* in several respects, have been described as members of the genus *Eulophidium* or have been transferred to it. A recent review of these species, and other species still allocated to *Eulophia*, has revealed that, in fact, two genera are represented. Several species have plicate leaves and pseudobulbs formed from several swollen nodes: these are retained as a section of *Eulophia*. But there is a group of thirty-one species which all have leathery leaves that are conduplicate, and commonly petiolate, and they arise above a pseudobulb formed by only a single swollen node. In this group the middle lobe of the three-lobed lip of the flower is often lobed, or emarginate at its apex, so that the complete lip looks four-lobed. Lindley's name, *Oeceoclades*, must be resurrected for all these species, because they include the plant on which he based the name and because it was published so much earlier than *Eulophidium*.

Oeceoclades lonchophylla is a widespread species that has itself received a number of different names. It was first collected in the Comoro Islands, and described as *Eulophia lonchophylla*. A few years later the German botanist, Rudolf Schlechter, described a specimen he collected himself in Mozambique as *Eulophia tainioides*. After a further fifty years Dr R.A. Dyer of Pretoria described specimens from the Lebombo Mountains in the south of Mozambique as *Eulophia dissimilis* or *Eulophidium dissimile*: he was uncertain in which genus the species should be classified. Summerhayes transferred all these names to the genus *Eulophidium* in 1957. In the most recent account, cited above, they are all placed in *Oeceoclades* and the conclusion is reached that they all represent a single widespread species. With the illustration here of a plant collected by Michael O'Connor at Mtunzini in Natal, and several other records of the occurrence of this species near Durban, it is now known from several shady, forest localities in south-eastern Africa, and in the adjacent Comoro Islands about 300 km offshore.

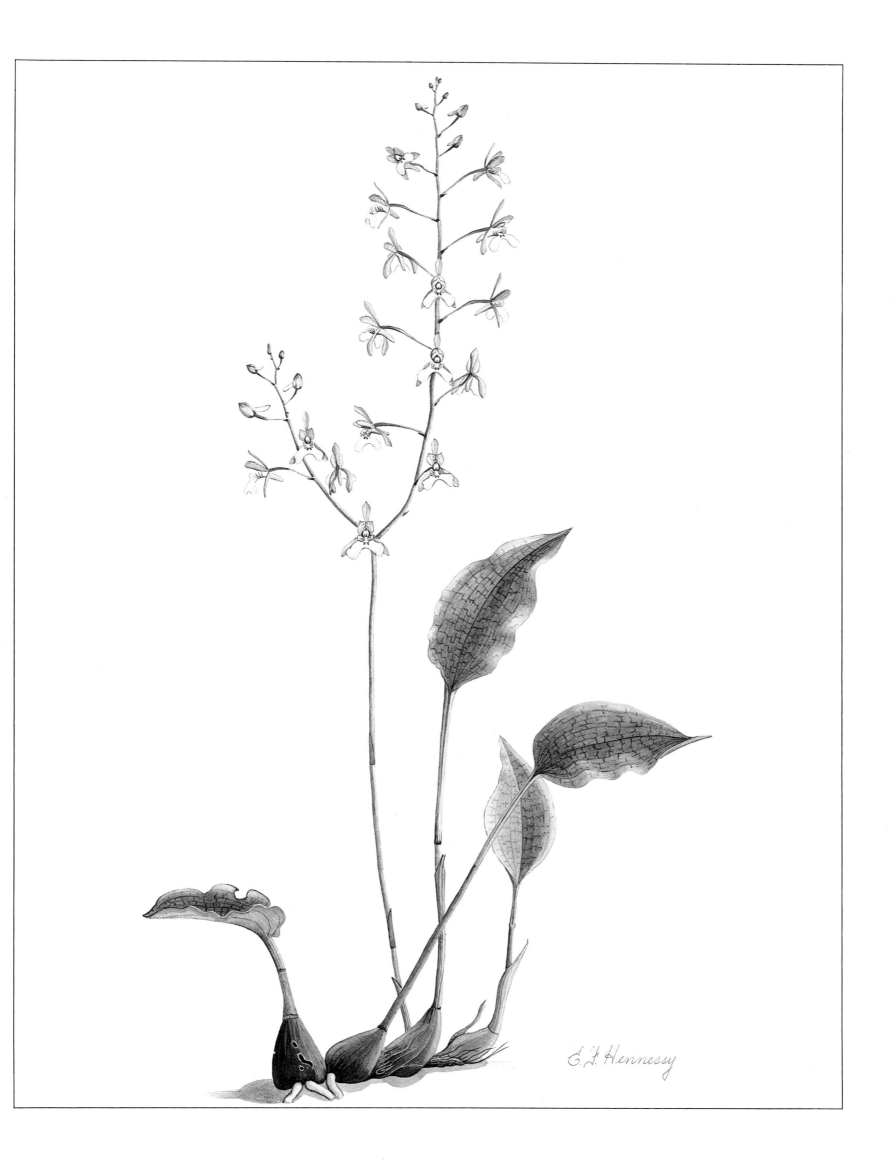

E. F. Hennessy

PLATE 49
Oeceoclades saundersiana

A handsome terrestrial species with vigorous growth and remarkable showy flowers. The large dark green pseudobulbs vary in length and width in different specimens, but are always borne above ground level and support one to three petiolate, glossy green leaves. The robust flower-spike grows up from the basal rhizome between the pseudobulbs and bears twenty to forty striking, dark-coloured flowers. The sepals are 1–2 cm long, narrower and distinctly longer than the petals, and often reflexed towards the ovary. All these parts are basically yellowish-green, but usually heavily overlaid with a dark purplish-brown and with even darker brownish veins. The lip is almost equally four-lobed, paler than the rest of the flower, but heavily veined in the same dark purplish-brown on either side of the creamy-green central patch that is situated immediately below the column. At the base of the lip there is a short greenish spur.

Plant life size

Oeceoclades saundersiana (Reichenbach *filius*) Garay and Taylor in *Botanical Museum Leaflets, Harvard University*, **24**: 270–271 (1976)
Eulophia saundersiana Reichenbach *filius* in *Botanische Zeitung*, **24**: 378 (1866)
Eulophidium saundersianum (Reichenbach *filius*) Summerhayes in *Bulletin du Jardin Botanique de l'État à Bruxelles*, **27**: 401 (1957)

The German Professor of Botany at the University of Hamburg, H.G. Reichenbach, first described this species from a pressed specimen sent to him by a prominent English orchid enthusiast, W. Wilson Saunders. Reichenbach mentioned, in the notes accompanying his description, that he had also seen one specimen of this species in the Kew Herbarium, which had probably been prepared from a plant sent to the Royal Botanic Gardens by the collector Gustav Mann, from West Africa. It seems likely that both specimens were part of the same importation, although their exact provenance is unknown.

The species is now known to be widely distributed in the tropical parts of Africa, from Sierra Leone in the west to Kenya in the east and as far south as Zambia and Angola. It is always found in rain-forest. In some of the drier parts of Africa there are only relict patches remaining, often forming a gallery of forest along streams and rivers. Here this *Oeceoclades* is frequently found as a stream-side plant, with its roots extending into the stream bed or floating in the water when the stream is full after rain.

The plant shown here was collected in Zambia and kindly loaned for illustration by Michael O'Connor, because the author's plants, which were collected in Kenya and Uganda, have refused to flower for several years. Usually, this is an easy species in cultivation. It requires slightly higher temperatures than the species described on the previous page, and grows better if it is more frequently and liberally supplied with water. Its large and spectacular flowers are unusually coloured, even in the orchid family, and they have a very pleasing shape.

A final feature of interest concerning the intriguing genus *Oeceoclades* relates to its distribution. Most species are confined to Madagascar, and several to Africa, the Mascarene or Seychelles islands, while some are variously distributed between these different land masses. There is one species that is believed to have been collected in India, but its exact locality is unknown. At the other extreme, another species, *O. maculata*, is widely distributed in the American continent. It occurs in Florida, in many of the islands in the Caribbean, and as far south as Bolivia and Argentina. An interesting point is that it is also widespread in the African continent. The second most widespread species is undoubtedly *O. saundersiana*.

E.F.Hennessy

PLATE 50
Ansellia africana

A robust epiphyte with tall stems, 50–100 cm long, that are slightly swollen to form cane-like pseudobulbs and arise close together in a dense clump. At the base of each stem thick roots attach it to the host branch and many thin upright roots make a conspicuous tuft surrounding the whole plant. In its upper part each pseudobulb bears six to twelve leathery leaves, neatly alternating in two distinct rows. As growth is completed, or up to a year later, an inflorescence arises at the apex of each cane. It may be simple or branched and bears up to a hundred flowers, sometimes more, each 3–5 cm in diameter. The perianth is thick and long-lasting, basically yellowish-green in colour but heavily overlaid with dark reddish-brown on its inner surface. These markings are also slightly evident on the pale outer surface of the flowers. The sepals are slightly longer, narrower and more pointed than the rounded petals. The lip is three-lobed: the striped basal lobes stand erect on either side of the stout column while the median lobe is a pure bright yellow and bears two parallel keels or ridges along its upper surface.

Plant x1/10; pseudobulb and flowers life size

Ansellia africana Lindley in *Edwards's Botanical Register*, **30**: t. 12 (1844)
Ansellia confusa N.E. Brown in *Lindenia*, **2**: 36 (1886)

Mature specimens of ansellia would easily qualify for the title of 'largest plant' in the orchid flora of Africa. Though of such tall growth, they are often dismissed as being of botanical, rather than horticultural value, 'useful for grouping with other subjects' but not striking in themselves. It is true that the flowers are only of modest size, but they are pleasantly scented during the day and are usually produced in great quantity. Flowering takes place in mid-winter, when there are many more showy orchid flowers available, and ansellias may have been unfairly judged on this account. The plant selected for the accompanying illustration bears rather few flowers but they have heavier and darker markings than any others we have seen.

The genus *Ansellia* was established by Lindley in honour of the gardener who first introduced it to England from the island of Fernando Po. John Ansell was sent by the Royal Horticultural Society as an assistant to Theodor Vogel, chief botanist on the Niger Expedition led by Captain H.D. Trotter in 1841. He was more fortunate than some members of the party, 'which was furnished with eight physicians, three steam-boats and the blessing of Queen Victoria and the Prince Consort', many of whom failed to return. Ansell's orchid, *A. africana*, is now known to occur throughout the hot equatorial region of Africa, from Liberia to western Kenya. It is always a forest plant, and grows only in very shady and humid positions.

In cultivation the black ansellia seems rather shy of producing its handsome and unusual flowers, compared with the fecundity and regularity of the yellow-flowered *A. gigantea*. The latter species occurs in the more brightly lit woodlands, and in the scattered trees of savanna country, throughout those parts of Africa that are subjected to a seasonal dry season, from northern Nigeria east to Kenya and thence south to Natal and Namibia. Many different forms can be recognised as distinct, by the shape and size of their flowers and by the density of the brown markings on the sepals and petals. Orchid growers who like this genus would be happier if each form was recognised as a distinct species, or variety, but taxonomists are more conservative. They regard the genus as consisting of only two species, which have different distributions, habitats and perianth shape. The variation in size and markings, which both species exhibit in some degree, is considered at present to have no taxonomic significance. In the past, however, at least six different names have been used in the orchid literature.

E F Hennessy

Glossary

The definitions of botanical terms that are given below are limited to the sense in which the words have been used in this book. Many of them would have slightly different, or broader meanings in a wider botanical context.

ABSCISSED: separated, used with reference to the separation of all or part of a leaf

ABSCISSION: detachment of a plant part, usually used with reference to a leaf

ACUMINATE: gradually tapering to a long slender point or acumen

ADVENTITIOUS BUDS: those produced abnormally, directly from the stem instead of in the axil of a leaf

ADVENTITIOUS ROOTS: those produced from a stem, rhizome or leaf

ANTHER: the pollen-bearing part of a stamen

ANTHER CAP: the outer deciduous cap, or case, which covers the pollinia

APEX: the tip of a leaf, bract or stem

APICAL: at the tip

APICULATE: ending abruptly in a short point

APPENDAGE: a part, usually small, that is attached to another part

AURICLE: a small lobe of a leaf or tepal that is ear-shaped

AXIL: the angle between the upper side of a leaf, branch or bract and the stem, or axis, from which it grows

AXILLARY: growing in an axil

AXIS: the central or main stem of a plant or inflorescence

BRACT: a small leaf, or leaf-like structure, in the axil of which a flower is borne

BUD: the immature state of a flower or stem

CALCARATE: carrying a spur

CALLOSITY: a protuberance on the surface of a flower, often irregular in shape, and leathery or hard

CALLUS (singular), CALLI (plural): a solid protuberance caused by a mass of cells

CAPSULE: a dry fruit that splits open at maturity to release its seeds

CAUDICLE: a stalk connecting the pollen masses to the viscidium, or gland, or uniting them

CAULINE: belonging to the stem or arising from it

CHLOROPLAST: the granule, or plastid, that contains green pigments

CILIATE: fringed with short hairs, like eyelashes, on the margin

CLAVATE: thickened at the end, club-shaped

CLAW: the narrow, stalk-like base of the petal or lip

CLONAL: derived from a single individual by the growth of buds or divisions

COLUMN: the central part of the orchid flower, formed by the union of the stamen, style and stigma

CONDUPLICATE: folded lengthwise, V-shaped in cross-section

CORDATE: heart-shaped

CORM: an enlarged, fleshy, stem base

CORTEX: the ground tissue between the outer covering, the epidermis, and the vascular tissue

CORTICAL: relating to the cortex, occupying this position

CREST: a ridge, usually on one of the tepals, often decorated or fringed

CRISPATE: having an irregular, curly margin

CRISPED: irregular and curling, usually applied to the margin of a leaf or tepal

DECIDUOUS: falling off at some stage in the life of the flower or plant; not evergreen

DECURRENT: when the edges of the leaf appear to continue to grow down the stem as raised ridges or lines

DEFLEXED: bent or turned sharply downwards

DEHISCENCE: a method of opening when ripe by splitting along distinct lines

DENTATE: having a row of tooth-like outgrowths along the margin

DISC: the upper surface of the lip, usually used for the central part of the upper surface

DORMANT: applied to parts which are not in active growth

DORSAL: relating to the back, or outer surface

DORSAL SEPAL: the intermediate, or odd sepal, usually at the back or upper side of the flower

ELLIPSOID: an elliptic solid

ELLIPTIC: shaped like an ellipse, narrowly oblong with regular, rounded ends

EMBRYO: the rudimentary plant still enclosed in the seed

ENDEMIC: confined to a region, or country, and not occurring naturally anywhere else

ENZYMATIC: a chemical reaction brought about or speeded up by an enzyme

ENZYME: a protein of complex chemical constitution, produced in living cells and capable of changing the rate of a chemical reaction; a biological catalyst

EPICHILE: the terminal part of the lip, used when it is distinct from the basal part

EPIDERMIS: the cellular skin or covering of a plant, often protected by a waxy outer covering or cuticle

EPILITHIC: growing on rocks

EPIPHYTE: a plant that grows on other plants but not as a parasite

EPIPHYTIC: relating to epiphytes

EQUITANT: folded lengthwise so that the base of each leaf enfolds the next

EXFOLIATION: breaking away in scales or flakes, peeling off

FERTILISATION: the fusion of the two gametes, sperm and egg cell, to form a new individual

FILIFORM: thread-like

FIMBRIATE: having the margin fringed with long narrow processes or appendages

FLEXUOUS: zigzag, bent alternately in opposite directions

FLORIFEROUS: producing many flowers

FOOT: a basal extension of the column

FUGACIOUS: falling off, or withering away, very quickly

FUNGICIDE: a fungus-destroying substance

FUNGUS (singular), FUNGI (plural): a living organism that lacks chlorophyll and obtains its nutrients by digesting dead or living organic matter

GALEATE: hollow and vaulted, like a helmet

GENUS (singular), GENERA (plural): the smallest natural group containing distinct species

GIBBOSITY: a swelling at the base of an organ

GLABROUS: smooth, completely lacking hairs, spines or other projections

GLANDULAR: possessing glands, secreting structures on the outer surface of an organ, often hair-like

GLAUCOUS: bluish-green

GLOBOSE: spherical, or nearly so

GYNOSTEMIUM: the column

HABIT: the general appearance of a plant, whether prostrate, erect, climbing, etc.

HERBACEOUS: describing plants of small size whose stems are not woody, often plants with annual stems from a perennial root

HYGROSCOPIC: able to enlarge or shrink on the application or removal of moisture

HYPHA (singular), HYPHAE (plural): cylindrical, thread-like branches of the body of a fungus

HYPOCHILE: the basal portion of the lip

INDUMENTUM: any covering, such as hairs, wool, scales, etc.

INFLORESCENCE: the arrangement of flowers on the flowering stem

INTERMEDIATE SEPAL: the dorsal, or odd sepal, usually uppermost in the flower

INTERNODE: the space or portion of stem between two nodes

INTERVALLATE: describing flowers or inflorescences that arise from the same point on the stem in several consecutive flowering seasons

KEEL: a median lengthwise ridge

KEIKI: a small plant arising from the stem of a mature plant

LABELLUM: the lip, or lowest petal of an orchid flower; usually held on the lower side of the flower and different in form from the two lateral petals

LACINIATE: with the edge cut into narrow lobes, frequently irregularly

LAMELLA (singular), LAMELLAE (plural): a thin, plate-like elevation

LAMINA: part of a leaf or petal that is expanded, usually thin and flat; the blade

LANCEOLATE: lance or spear-shaped; much longer than wide and tapering to a point at both ends

LATERAL SEPALS: the pair of similar sepals arranged at the sides of the orchid flower

LAX: loose or distant, as opposed to tightly or densely arranged

LIANA: a very elongated climber, usually with a woody stem

LIGULATE: strap-shaped

LIMB: the broad or expanded part of a petal or leaf

LINEAR: narrow, many times longer than wide, sides parallel

LIP: the labellum, or odd petal of an orchid flower; usually held on the lower side of the flower and different in shape, colour and size from the two lateral petals

LITHOPHYTE: living on a rock

LOBE: a division of an organ, often round but may be of any shape

LOBULE: a small lobe

MASSULA (singular), MASSULAE (plural): a small group of pollen grains that remain stuck together

MENTUM: a chin-like projection formed at the base of the lip or by the united bases of the lateral sepals

MERISTEM: a group of unspecialised cells capable of division and becoming specialised to form new tissues of the plant

MESOCHILE: the intermediate part of the lip in those orchid flowers where three parts are clearly recognisable

MONILIFORM: like a string of beads

MONOCOTYLEDONS: plants characterised by one seed-leaf in the embryo, and other associated features

MONOPODIAL: a stem with a single, continuous axis

MYCELIUM: the vegetative growth of a fungus, made up of many hyphae

MYCORRHIZA, MYCORRHIZAL: the symbiotic union of a fungus with the roots of a plant

NECTAR: a sweet fluid secreted by various parts of a plant, frequently by a part of the flower

NECTAR GUIDE: lines of colour on the sepals and petals which indicate the position of the nectary

NECTARIFEROUS: nectar-bearing

NECTARY: the organ in which nectar is secreted

NODE: a point on the stem where a leaf is attached

NON-RESUPINATE: the pedicel and ovary not twisted so that the lip is on the upper side of the flower

OSMOPHORE: tissue that is scent-producing

OVARY: that part of the flower which contains the ovules; an immature fruit

OVATE: egg-shaped in outline, usually pointed at the apex

OVULE: the organ in the ovary which develops into a seed after fertilisation

PALMATE: divided into lobes or segments like the palm of a hand

PANICLE: a branching inflorescence in which all the branches bear flowers

PANICULATE: flowers arranged as in a panicle

PAPILLA (singular), PAPILLAE (plural): small, fleshy protuberance on the surface of leaf or flower

PAPILLOSE: bearing papillae

PARASITE: an organism that lives directly on another living organism

PEDICEL: the stalk of an individual flower

PEDUNCLE: the stalk of an inflorescence

PERENNATION: survival from one year to another

PERENNIAL: lasting for several years

PERIANTH: the colourful parts of the orchid flower, consisting of six tepals usually distinguished as three sepals, two petals and the lip

PETALS: two of the three inner members of the perianth in orchid flowers

PETIOLE: the stalk of a leaf

PETIOLATE: having a petiole

PHEROMONES: chemicals used in communication between the individuals of a particular species of insect; often a sex attractant

PHOTOSYNTHESIS: process by which the energy of sunlight is captured by the green pigments of plants and used to build up complex materials from water and carbon dioxide

PHYTOALEXIN: antibiotic substances produced by plants as a response to infection

PLACENTA: the part of the ovary to which the ovules are attached

PLICATE: folded like a fan; pleated

PNEUMATHODE: an opening in a root through which gaseous exchange can take place

POLLEN: the individual grains produced in the anther, which, on germination, produce a pollen tube containing the male gamete, or sperm cell

POLLINARIUM: the entire pollen-bearing structure of the orchid flower, including viscidium and stipe, caudicles and pollinia, which is usually transported in one piece by the pollinating insect

POLLINATION: the deposition of pollen on the stigmatic surface of the flower

POLLINIUM (singular), POLLINIA (plural): a body composed of many pollen grains cohering together

PROTOCORM: the first stage of development of the orchid seed

PSEUDOBULB: the thickened stem or stem-base of many orchid plants

PSEUDOCOPULATION: erratic movements performed by male insects on certain orchid flowers

PSEUDOPOLLEN: yellow cells or groups of cells on the surface of the lip which resemble superficially the pollen of other flowers

RACEME: an unbranched inflorescence in which the flowers are borne on short pedicels and usually open in succession from the base upwards

RACHIS: the flower-bearing portion of an inflorescence

RADICAL: describing leaves which arise so close to the base of the stem as to appear to be proceeding from the root

RECURVED: curved downwards or back upon itself

RESUPINATE: having the lip lowermost because the pedicel or ovary is twisted through 180°

RETICULATE: net-veined; the smallest visible veins are connected like the meshes of a net

RHIZOME: a root-like stem that creeps under or over the ground or other surface, sending roots downwards, and branches, leaves or flowering shoots upwards; always distinguished from a root by the presence of leaves or scales and buds

ROSTELLUM: a projection from the upper edge of the stigma in front of the anther

SACCATE: pouched or bag-shaped

SAPROPHYTE: a living organism that obtains its nourishment from dead organic matter

SCAPE: a leafless flower-stalk arising from the ground

SECUND: with the flowers arranged apparently in one row along the side of an inflorescence

SEPALS: the three outermost tepals of the perianth of the flower

SESSILE: without a stalk

SHEATH: the lower portion of the leaf, clasping the stem; also used for bracts which enclose the flowering stem below those which support the flowers

SINUS: the curve or space between two lobes of a leaf

SPECIES: a group of individuals that exhibit the same distinctive characters; the unit which provides the basis for classification

SPIKE: an unbranched inflorescence bearing sessile flowers

SPREADING: arranged so that the tips of the parts are directed outwards, more or less horizontally

SPUR: a tubular projection from one of the floral parts, usually the lip or the dorsal sepal

STAMEN: the male organ of the flower, consisting of only an anther in African orchids

STAMINODE: a sterile stamen; a structure appearing in the place of a stamen but bearing no pollen

STELE: a central cylinder of specialised tissues through which water and dissolved substances are transported within the root

STELIDIUM (singular), STELIDIA (plural): a term used to describe two small teeth at the apex of the column in certain genera of orchids

STIGMA, STIGMATIC SURFACE: the sticky area that receives the pollen or pollinarium

STIPE: the stalk that connects the viscidium with the caudicles of the pollinia

STOLON: a branch which, because it roots at a node, often gives rise to a new individual at some distance from the parent plant

SUBTRIBE: a small group of genera that have certain characteristics in common; a smaller unit of classification than the tribe

SUBULATE: with a fine, sharp point; awl-shaped

SUPERPOSED: arranged vertically, each somewhat above the preceding

SYMBIOSIS: the living together of dissimilar organisms with benefit to one or both

SYMBIOTIC: relating to symbiosis

SYMPODIAL: a stem made up of a series of superposed branches; each branch terminates in a leaf or flower and a new branch arises below it to extend the body of the plant

SYNONYM: another name for the same species or genus, but one which is no longer in general use

TAXONOMIST: one who is skilled in classification

TAXONOMIC: pertaining to classification

TEPAL: a division of the perianth; usually used collectively or when the perianth is not markedly differentiated into sepals and petals

TERETE: cylindrical, circular in cross-section

TERRESTRIAL: on or in the ground

TRIBE: a group of several genera that have certain characteristics in common

TUBER: (1) a thickened branch of an underground stem, which produces buds; (2) a swollen root or branch of a root which serves as a store of reserve food

TUFTED: a group of leaves arising very close together at the base

UMBEL: an inflorescence in which the diverging pedicels, all of the same length, arise from the same point at the apex of the peduncle

UNDULATE: with a wavy margin or surface

VANDACEOUS: with a habit of growth similar to that of the genus *Vanda*, i.e. monopodial, with the leaves in two ranks

VASCULAR: containing specialised cells for the conduction of water or sap

VELAMEN: the absorbent epidermis of the roots of many orchids

VENATION: the arrangement of the veins in a leaf, bract or flower

VERRUCOSE: warty

VESTIGIAL: degenerate or imperfectly developed

VISCIDIUM (singular), VISCIDIA (plural): the sticky gland attached to the pollinium, usually produced by the rostellum

WHORL: parts arranged in a circle around an axis

Bibliography

In addition to the original descriptions of each of the selected species, which are cited on the relevant pages, we have obtained some of the information included in this book from the sources given below. All other data have been derived from our own observations.

Arditti, J. (1966). Orchids. *Scientific American*, **214**(1): 70–78.

Ball, J.S. (1978). *Southern African Epiphytic Orchids*. Conservation Press, Johannesburg.

Bolus, H. (1918). *The Orchids of the Cape Peninsula*, 2nd ed., ed. H.M.L. Bolus and A.M. Greene. Darter Brothers and Company, Cape Town.

Coats, A.M. (1969). *The Quest for Plants*. Studio Vista, London.

Cribb, P.J. (1977). New Orchids from South Central Africa. *Kew Bulletin,* **32**: 137–187.

Cribb, P.J. (1978). A revision of *Stolzia (Orchidaceae)*. *Kew Bulletin*, **33**: 79–89.

Cribb, P.J. (1978). A synopsis of *Malaxis (Orchidaceae)* in Africa. *Kew Bulletin*, **32**: 737–741.

Cribb, P.J. (1979). New or little-known orchids from East Africa. *Kew Bulletin*, **34**: 321–340.

Darnell, A.W. (1930). *Orchids for the Outdoor Garden*. L. Reeve and Company, Ashford, Kent.

Darwin, C. (1877). *The various contrivances by which orchids are fertilised by insects*, 2nd ed., John Murray, London.

Desmond, R. (1977). *Dictionary of British and Irish Botanists and Horticulturists*. Taylor and Francis, London.

Dockrill, A.W. (1969). *Australian Indigenous Orchids*. The Society for Growing Australian Plants.

Dressler, R.L. (1974). Classification of the Orchid Family. *Proceedings of the 7th World Orchid Conference 1974*, 259–278.

Duckitt, F. (1977). Satyriums and their culture. *South African Orchid Journal*, **8**: 121–125.

Fisch, M.H., Shechter, Y. and Arditti, J. (1972). Orchids and the Discovery of Phytoalexins. *American Orchid Society Bulletin*, **41**: 605–607.

Garay, L.A. and Taylor, P. (1976). The genus *Oeceoclades* Lindl. *Botanical Museum Leaflets, Harvard University*, **24**: 249–274.

Grosvenor, R.K. (1976). A list of orchids indigenous in Rhodesia. *Excelsa*, **6**: 76–86.

Hall, A.V. (1965). Studies of the South African Species of *Eulophia*. *Journal of South African Botany*, Supplementary Vol. No. V.

Harrison, E.R. (1972). *Epiphytic Orchids of Southern Africa*. Natal Branch of the Wildlife Protection and Conservation Society of South Africa, Durban, South Africa.

Harvey, W.H. (1863). *Thesaurus Capensis* 2. Hodges, Smith and Company, Dublin.

Henrey, B. (1975). *British Botanical and Horticultural Literature before 1800*. 3 vols. Oxford University Press, Oxford.

Hepper, F.N. and Neate, F. (1971). Plant Collectors in west Africa. *Regnum Vegetabile*, **74**.

Holman, R.T. and Heimermann, W.H. (1973). Identification of Components of Orchid Fragrance by Gas Chromatography — Mass Spectrometry. *American Orchid Society Bulletin*, **42**: 678–682.

Hooker, J.D. (1870). *Stenoglottis fimbriata*. *Curtis's Botanical Magazine*, **96**: t. 5872.

Hooker, J.D. (1880). *Pachystoma ? thomsonianum*. *Curtis's Botanical Magazine*, **106**: t. 6471.

Hooker, J.D. (1880). *Disa megaceras*. *Curtis's Botanical Magazine*, **106**: t. 6529.

Hooker, J.D. (1891). *Stenoglottis longifolia*. *Curtis's Botanical Magazine*, **117**: t. 7186.

Hooker, J.D. (1895). *Bartholina pectinata*. *Curtis's Botanical Magazine*, **121**: t. 7450.

Hooker, W.J. (1839). *Polystachya grandiflora*. *Curtis's Botanical Magazine*, **65**: t. 3707.

Hooker, W.J. (1844). *Disa grandiflora*. *Curtis's Botanical Magazine*, **70**: t. 4073.

Hooker, W.J. (1845). *Polystachya bracteosa*. *Curtis's Botanical Magazine*, **71**: t. 4161.

Hooker, W.J. (1857). *Ansellia africana. Curtis's Botanical Magazine*, **83**: t. 4965.

Hunt, P.F. and Grierson, M.A. (1973). *Orchidaceae*. The Bourton Press, England.

Johansson, D. (1974). Ecology of vascular epiphytes in West African rain forest. *Acta Phytogeographica Suecica*, **59**, Uppsala.

Johnson, K.C. (1967). *Disa uniflora* — a method of cultivation and its hybridisation with *D. racemosa. Journal of the Botanical Society of South Africa*, **53**: 19–26.

Jonsson, L. (1979). New combinations in the African genera *Chauliodon* and *Solenangis* (Orchidaceae). *Botaniska Notiser*, **132**: 381–384.

Keay, R.W.J. (1954). *Flora of West Tropical Africa*, 2nd ed., Vol. I (1). Introduction. Crown Agents for Oversea Governments and Administrations, London.

Lighton, C. (1973). *Cape Floral Kingdom*. Juta, Cape Town.

Lindquist, B. (1965). The raising of *Disa uniflora* seedlings in Gothenburg. *American Orchid Society Bulletin*, **34**: 317–319.

Millar, A. (1978). *Orchids of Papua New Guinea: an Introduction*. University of Washington Press, Seattle and London.

Morris, B. (1970). *The Epiphytic Orchids of Malawi*. The Society of Malawi, Blantyre.

Nicholls, W.H. (1969). *Orchids of Australia*. Nelson, London.

Nihoul, E., Schelpe, E.A. and Hunt, P.F. (1969). A provisional checklist of the orchids in the Congo-Kinshasa. *American Orchid Society Bulletin*, **38**: 578–584.

Piers, F. (1968). *Orchids of East Africa*. J. Cramer, Lehre.

Podzorski, A.C. and Cribb, P.J. (1979). A revision of *Polystacha* sect. *Cultriformes (Orchidaceae). Kew Bulletin*, **34**: 147–186.

Rasmussen, F.N. (1974). *Diaphananthe adoxa* sp. nov. (Orchidaceae) from southern Ethiopia and the inclusion of *Sarcorhynchus* in *Diaphananthe. Norwegian Journal of Botany*, **21**: 227–232.

Rayner, E. (1977). Orchids as medicine. *South African Orchid Journal*, **8**(4): 120.

Reinikka, M.A. (1972). *A History of the Orchid*. University of Miami Press, Coral Gables, Florida.

Richter, W. (1965). *The Orchid World*. Studio Vista, London.

Rolfe, R.A. (1897–98). Orchideae, in W.T. Thiselton-Dyer (ed.), *Flora of Tropical Africa*, **7**: 12–292. L. Reeve and Company, Ashford.

Rolfe, R.A. (1907). *Angraecum infundibulare. Curtis's Botanical Magazine*, **133**: t. 8153.

Rolfe, R.A. (1912–1913). Orchideae, in W.T. Thiselton-Dyer (ed.), *Flora Capensis*, **5**(3): 3–313. L. Reeve and Company, London.

Sanford, W.W. and Adanlawo, I. (1973). Velamen and exodermis characters of West African epiphytic orchids in relation to taxonomic grouping and habitat tolerance. *Botanical Journal of the Linnean Society*, **66**: 307–321.

Schelpe, E.A. (1966). *An Introduction to the South African Orchids*. Purnell and Sons, Cape Town.

Schelpe, E.A. (1968). Disa hybrids. *Journal of the Botanical Society of South Africa*, **54**: 34–35.

Schelpe, E.A. (1969). *Disperis capensis. Flowering Plants of Africa*, **40**: Plate 1573.

Schelpe, E.A. (1976). The Early History of South African Orchidology. *South African Orchid Journal*, **7**: 77–80.

Schultes, R.E. and Pease, A.S. (1963). *Generic Names of Orchids: Their Origin and Meaning*. Academic Press. New York and London.

Sims, J. (1812). *Satyrium carneum. Curtis's Botanical Magazine*, **37**: t. 1512.

Stafleu, F.A. (1967). *Taxonomic Literature. Regnum Vegetabile*, **52**.

Stafleu, F.A. and Cowan, R.S. (1976). *Taxonomic Literature* Vol. I. A-G. *Regnum Vegetabile*, **94**.

Stafleu, F.A. and Cowan, R.S. (1979). *Taxonomic Literature* Vol. II: H-Le. *Regnum Vegetabile*, **98**.

Stewart, J. (1973). A second checklist of the orchids of Kenya. *American Orchid Society Bulletin*, **42**: 525–531.

Stewart, J. (1974). Orchidaceae, in A.D.Q. Agnew (ed.) *Upland Kenya Wild Flowers*: 726–802. Oxford University Press, Oxford.

Stewart, J. (1976). The Vandaceous group in Africa and Madagascar. *Proceedings of the 8th World Orchid Conference* 1975: 239–248.

Stewart, J. (1979). A revision of the African species of *Aerangis* (Orchidaceae). *Kew Bulletin*, **34**(2): 239–319.

Stewart, J. and Campbell, B. (1970). *Orchids of Tropical Africa*. W.H. Allen, London.

Stewart, J. and Hennessy, E.F. (1980). *Didymoplexis verrucosa* — a new saprophytic orchid from South Africa. *American Orchid Society Bulletin*, **49**: 836–842.

Stoutamire, W. (1974). Terrestrial Orchid Seedlings, in C.L. Withner (ed.), *The Orchids: Scientific Studies*, 101–128. John Wiley, New York.

Summerhayes, V.S. (1936). African Orchids VIII. *Kew Bulletin* **1936**: 221–233.

Summerhayes, V.S. (1937). African Orchids IX. *Kew Bulletin* **1937**: 457–466.

Summerhayes, V.S. (1938). African Orchids X. *Kew Bulletin* **1938**: 141–153.

Summerhayes, V.S. (1942). African Orchids XII. *Botanical Museum Leaflets, Harvard University*, **10**: 257–299.

Summerhayes, V.S. (1948). African Orchids XVIII. *Kew Bulletin*, **3**: 277–302.

Summerhayes, V.S. (1949). African Orchids XIX. *Kew Bulletin*, **4**: 427–443.

Summerhayes, V.S. (1957). African Orchids XXIV. *Kew Bulletin*, **12**: 107–126.

Summerhayes, V.S. (1958). African Orchids XXVI. *Kew Bulletin*, **13**: 257–281.

Summerhayes, V.S. (1960). African Orchids XXVII. *Kew Bulletin*, **14**: 126–157.

Summerhayes, V.S. (1966). African Orchids XXX. *Kew Bulletin*, **20**: 165–199.

Summerhayes, V.S. (1968a). Orchidaceae, in F.N. Hepper (ed.), *Flora of West Tropical Africa*, 2nd ed., **3**(1): 180–276. Crown Agents for Oversea Governments and Administrations, London.

Summerhayes, V.S. (1968b). Orchidaceae (Part 1), in E. Milne-Redhead and R.M. Polhill (eds.), *Flora of Tropical East Africa*. Crown Agents for Oversea Governments and Administrations, London.

Summerhayes, V.S. and Hall, A.V. (1962). The type species and conservation of the generic name *Eulophia* R. Br. ex Lindl. *Taxon*, **11**: 201–203.

Van der Pijl, L. and Dodson, C.H. (1966). *Orchid Flowers: Their Pollination and Evolution*. The Fairchild Tropical Garden and the University of Miami Press.

Veitch, H.J. (1891). *A Manual of Orchidaceous Plants*, Part VII. James Veitch and Sons, Chelsea.

Williams, B.S. and H., (1894). *The Orchid Grower's Manual*, 7th ed., London.

Williamson, G. (1977). *The Orchids of South Central Africa*. J.M. Dent, London.

Withner, C.L. (1974). *The Orchids: Scientific Studies*. John Wiley and Sons, New York.

Index to the Plates

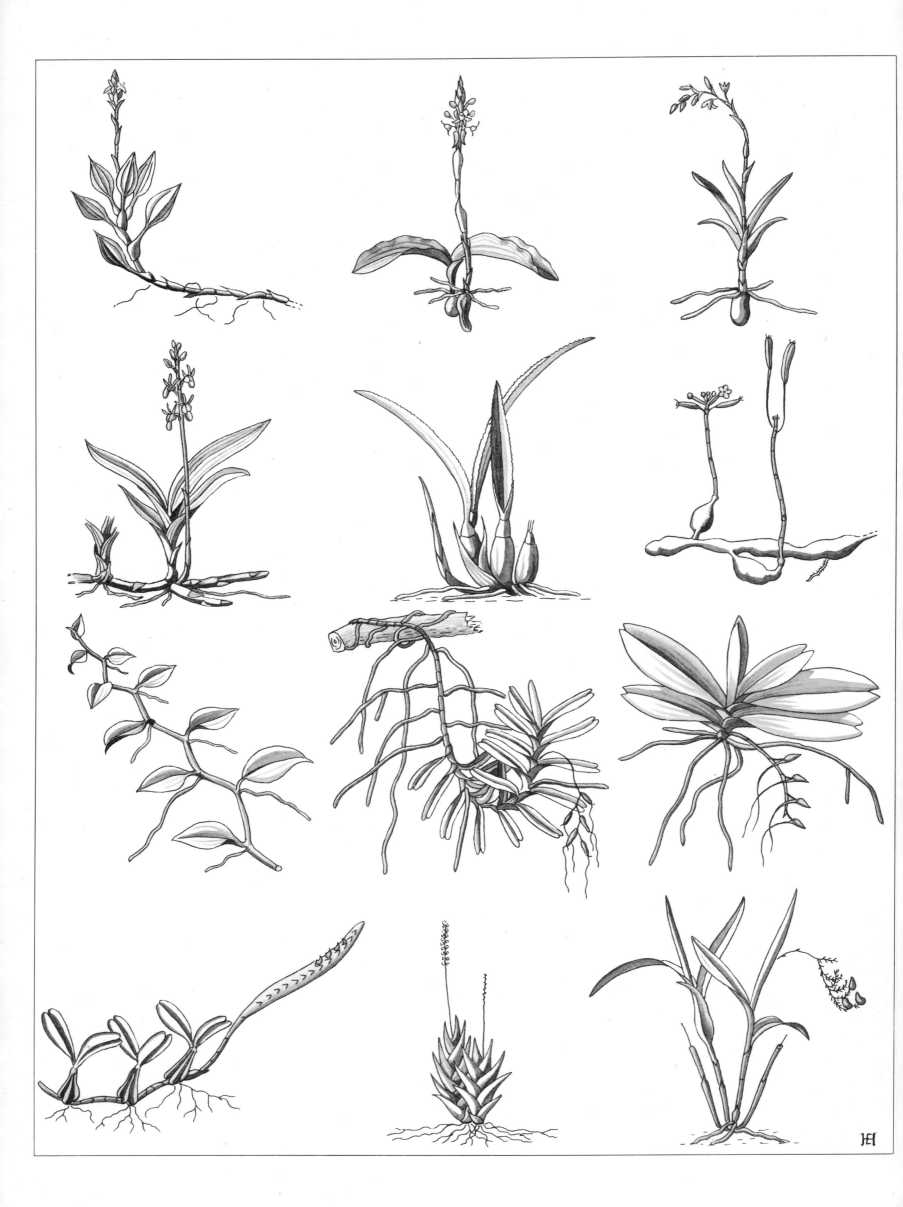